FIELD DRESSING YOUR BIG GAME

caribou • deer • moose

FIELD DRESSING YOUR BIG GAME

caribou • deer • moose

R.M. LeMay

www.rmlemay.com

Collaborators

Special participation:
Alain Demers

Photographers:
Quebec, ministère de la Faune et des Parcs
Pierre Bernier, Didier LeHenaff
Roger Fortier
John Taylor
Andrew Taylor
Guy Charrette
Robert Laplante
Yvon-Louis Paquet
R.M. LeMay

Illustrations:
Richard Brillon

Translation:
George Gruenefeld

Coordination:
Karol Lefebvre

Graphic design and prepress:
Adhoc

FIELD DRESSING YOUR BIG GAME

Copyright © Editions R. M. LeMay Inc. 2005

Legal deposit 2nd trimester 2005
Bibliothèque nationale du Québec
National Library of Canada

Printed by H.L.N.
Sherbrooke, Qc. Canada

ISBN 0-9738619-0-8

I dedicate this book to all the novice hunters who, for the first time in their lives, will experience the excitement of a hunting season opening this fall.

Good hunting

Acknowledgements

The publication of this book was made possible thanks to the help of several people and I would be remiss to not mention the encouragement and support they provided throughout the project.

First of all, I want to express my gratitude to Roger Fortier for his confidence in my project as well as to my father, Lucien LeMay, my sisters Monique and Suzanne LeMay and to my friend and hunting companion, Guy Charrette. I also want to say thank you to Alain Demers for his participation. The same goes for John Taylor and Yvon-Louis Paquet.

Likewise, I'm indebted to George Gruenefeld for his work and valuable advice. And for their help Luiza Matoso, Robert Buttars and Richard Oliver. Also to Raymond Himbault of Himbault Gibier.

In addition, I would like to thank Wedge Hills Outfitter operating out of Schefferville and SEPAQ on Anticosti Island. Lachance Hunting and Fishing in Sherbrooke was kind enough to lend me some of the equipment illustrated in this book.

And last, but not least, I want to thank Karol Lefebvre who provided the unflinching encouragement and invaluable advice from start to finish.

Meet the author

As far back as he can remember, Réjean M. LeMay recalls following his father when he went small game hunting. In the process, he not only developed a love for the sport but also a deep respect for the game and the discipline required to properly care for it after the shot. As a teenager, he worked in his father's butcher shop to learn the basics of the trade and was soon able to earn a living from it.

In 1974, Réjean enrolled in the National Meat Institute to improve his knowledge of meat cutting and master the trade. Then, after working as a butcher for a number of years, he returned to the Institute for additional courses on special cutting techniques. During this time, he caught the attention of the management and they invited him to join the teaching staff of the Institute. In 1978, at the age of 24, Réjean officially became a retail butchery teacher.

Réjean holds a bachelor's degree in teaching and, in addition to teaching, he frequently gives workshops and seminars on buying and preserving retail meat cuts. He also does radio and television appearances on the subjects of both meat handling and the outdoors.

Réjean has also written a regular column on meat handling for a monthly magazine on food and has co-authored two books on big game. He has also taught firearms safety courses for over a decade as well as courses on the care and preservation of game and fish. He is frequently called upon as an expert by the government to identify meat seized from poachers.

In addition, Réjean has worked with the Inuit of northern Canada to establish and operate a caribou slaughter house and meat processing plant.

An angler and hunter at heart, he still manages to spend every free moment in the outdoors. His passion for big game hunting allows him to try different techniques and test new theories concerning the preservation and storage of venison. Whether it's deer, moose or caribou, Réjean's 35 years of experience in the field stand him in good stead to derive every last ounce from his hunts.

Table of contents

Introduction 15

CHAPTER 1

Vital zones & recovering game 17
Aim for the right target .17
The art of tracking 19
Recovering an animal underwater 22

CHAPTER 2

Too good to waste 27
Delayed field dressing .27
Air circulation 28
Heat 29
Skin on, skin off 33
On the hood 35
Questionable methods .36
Practical advice 36
   Reasonable return .36
   Deer 38

CHAPTER 3

The tenderness factor 39
Ante mortem conditions 39
Deer & caribou 41
Post mortem conditions 42
Storage 43
Aging period 44

CHAPTER 4

Tools & accessories **45**
Knives 45
Sharpening stones 52
Axes 56
Saws 58
Ropes 58
Cheesecloth bags 60
Peach paper 61
Rain pants 61
Gloves 61
Others 61

CHAPTER 5

Field dressing
Bleeding 65
Prior to field dressing 66
The organ meats 67
Steps to follow 68
   Caribou 73
   Deer 80
   Moose 86
Practical advice 91

CHAPTER 6

Quartering **93**
Removing the head 97
Four quarters 97
   Caribou 99
   Moose 104
A lighter load 106
Carrying them out 109
Practical advice 111

CHAPTER 7

Variety meats **115**
The recipes 119

CHAPTER 8

Transporting the meat **121**
Preparing the front sections 121
Preparing the legs 124
Preparing the full loins .126

CHAPTER 9

Parasites & diseases **129**
Tapeworm 129
Liver flukes 130
Hidatid cysts 130
Warble fly 130
Tuberculosis 130
Abscesses 132
Warts 132
Chronic wasting disease 132
Cadmium 132
Government agencies 133

CHAPTER 10

Your trophy **135**
The head 135
The antlers 137

Conclusion **141**

Introduction

Back in the days when our distant ancestors still lived in caves, long before the concept of making electricity was even a remote hope and when game was still abundant, the task of keeping meat from decomposing must have been an ongoing challenge. Granted, the freezing temperatures through the long winters may have extended the best-before date of their provisions to some degree, but archaeologists suggest that other methods of conserving meat — brining, drying and smoking — were likely the result of happy accidents rather than premeditation. Although we have improved on the basics and fine-tuned the concepts, the fact remains that the methods developed many, many millennia ago by those early hunters are still widely used today.

Here in North America, the first European settlers relied heavily on the vast forests to provide meat for the table. What few cattle were available were used in breeding and expanding the meager herds and, as such, were far too valuable a commodity to be slaughtered for the table. Remember that, in those days, everything was brought by boat from Europe, livestock included.

The pioneers hunted deer, moose, elk and caribou out of necessity and the trade in furs provided income, clothing and even food (muskrat, beaver, etc.). They had no imposed seasons but rather their harvests were guided by the time of year, the migrations and the abundance of game. It was only centuries later, during the early 1900s, when the first wildlife conservation measures were formally enacted.

Today, perhaps with the exception of native North Americans living in remote areas, we are no longer forced to hunt for subsistence. Most people now consider hunting to be a sport or a form of recreation. It has become largely a family

15

tradition in which the heritage and the love for the days spent afield are passed on from generation to generation. In addition, the ranks of hunters expand even further with the arrival of newcomers who are curious about this age-old activity.

The attraction, no, the magic of hunting is that not only does it provide us with unforgettable days spent in the forests, but also with an abundance of outstanding venison. Deer, elk, moose and caribou are not just game animals, they are the main ingredients of happy meals shared with family and friends, provided the meat has been properly cared for and prepared. That process starts the moment after we pull the trigger. From the moment we locate our game, a series of precautions need to be followed so that we can derive the maximum benefit from it.

This book contains a wealth of information to help you get both the best quality meat and the optimum quantity from the animal you have harvested. Packed full with explanations, colour photos and illustrations, it covers all the means and techniques that ensure you will get the most out of your experience. Accuracy, vital zones, the choice of animal for the best quality meat, the care of the meat as well as the best tools to use and an understanding of the animal's bone structure are just some of the considerations that will minimize the loss of meat. In addition, there is a chapter on organ meats, another on the various diseases to be aware of and, last but not least, several pages of advice on having your trophy mounted.

All of the techniques and gems of advice provided in this book are applicable to all big game animals found in North America including whitetailed deer, mule deer, blacktailed and Sitka deer, pronghorn antelope, elk, moose and caribou as well as most of the introduced species, including fallow deer and red deer.

Chapter 1

Vital zones & recovering game

The best way to quickly and humanely dispatch your game is to carefully aim for and hit one of the vital zones (see diagram next page). It will make your task of field dressing and cleaning the animal much easier.

Aim for the right target

Regardless of the distance, you cannot go wrong by aiming for the chest. The ideal point of impact is between one half and one third the way up along an imaginary line drawn through the chest cavity immediately behind the front leg. The heart is located in the forward portion of the chest and is concealed behind the lower shoulder muscles of the front leg. The liver is located toward the back end of the chest cavity between the seventh and tenth ribs. The lungs are highly vulnerable organs that fill most of the thorax and therefore represent a large target.

There are actually two advantages to aiming for the chest cavity. First, the chances of recovering the animal quickly are excellent. Second, there is virtually no loss of meat when the animal is hit in the chest. So, when the animal is standing broadside, take your time, aim carefully and squeeze the trigger smoothly.

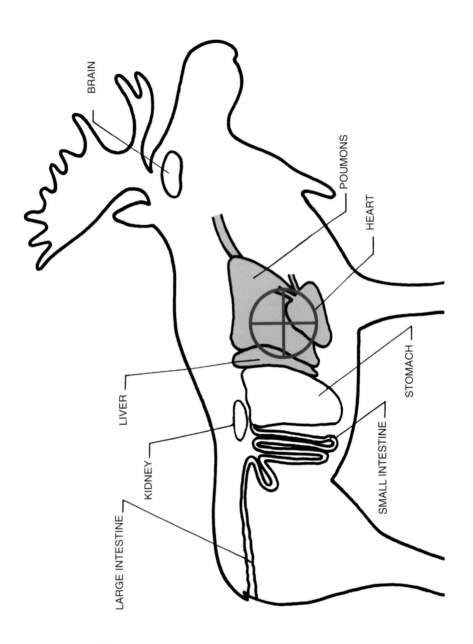

The vital zones

The shaded areas show the three major vital areas of an animal that hunters should aim for.

A face-on target is considerably more difficult, but equally deadly. If the animal's head is up, aim for the center of the chest and squeeze off a well-placed shot.

If you are close to the animal and are a competent marksman, another option is to aim for the head or, more accurately, a point behind the eye at the point of the ear channel in order to penetrate the brain cavity. Most other areas of the head are protected by dense bone which can and often does deflect the bullet.

A neck shot can be extremely efficient if it is executed accurately. However, the spinal column is a relatively small target which can be easily missed.

Avoid shooting at an animal with its tail to you because the chances of dropping it quickly are slim. Even if you do hit your target, the projectile will primarily damage the intestines, causing drawn-out suffering that can last hours and even days. More often than not, an animal shot in this way will be lost. If you are lucky enough to find the animal, a large amount of meat will have been ruined. You are much better off waiting a few moments longer in the hopes that a shot into the chest cavity presents itself.

A favourite target for moose hunters is the hump of the back. It is a vital target inasmuch as the shot may fracture or cause a dislocation of the spinal column which, in turn, results in damage to the spinal cord, paralysing the animal. However, if your shot is even slightly off target, your bullet will bury itself in muscle tissue without even slowing down the animal.

The art of tracking

More than any other, big game hunting demands a large measure of self-discipline and steady nerves, especially when an injured animal escapes. Inexperienced hunters have the tendency to immediately take off in pursuit of the animal out of fear of losing it. In actual fact, this hasty response increases the odds that the animal will not be found.

Members of the deer family – including moose, elk and caribou – have a great deal of stamina when injured, allowing them to run for surprising distances. Any animal that senses it is being followed will continue fleeing until it feels that it is no longer in danger or until it succumbs to the injuries. It will usually try to work its way back to a safe haven and such areas are often extremely difficult to find and enter.

Naturally, an animal hit in the primary vital zones – the head, the heart or the spinal column – will usually collapse in its tracks. On the other hand, an animal that has been hit in the lungs, the liver or, if a major artery has been cut, will often have enough strength to flee. The distance will depend on the degree of this injury. Even worse, an animal hit in the intestines can mean difficult tracking lasting many hours. Finally, a shot that enters the muscle tissue without cutting major veins or arteries can be almost impossible to recover. Unfortunately, these kinds of injuries are rarely fatal and game butchers frequently discover evidence of past bullets or arrow damage while butchering animals.

With this in mind, resist the temptation to follow the fleeing animal immediately after the shot, no matter what the time of day. Rather, give it time to bed down and stiffen as a result of its injury. A minimum of 30 minutes is a good rule of thumb if you are hunting with a rifle, and 60 minutes should be the minimum for bowhunters. This gives the tissues an opportunity to become numb and stiff, making it easier for the hunter to then recover the animal, often just a short distance from where it was hit.

The amount and colour of blood the animal loses in the course of its escape, as well as how it is distributed on the ground and vegetation are extremely important clues as to where and how badly the animal has been hit. A good hunter must be able to read these clues quickly and accurately in order to recover the game.

A steady trail of dark blood indicates that a major blood vessel has been damaged. The animal will not go far, so sit back, be patient and listen. Small drops of light-coloured blood down the centre of the track means that the animal has been hit in the lungs (photo 1.1). In this case, examine the branches and vegetation at about thigh height and you will likely spot tiny spots of blood as if they had been sprayed with a painter's spray gun.

An animal hit in the upper portion of the intestines will not likely leave much of a trail other than occasional drops of clear blood. On the other hand, if the animal has been hit in the lower portion of the intestines, you will probably find a substantial trail of dark blood, often with small bits of plant fibre mixed in. At first, you will likely find drops about the size of a pea and some small pools of blood. While tracking the animal, be as quiet and careful as you can.

If the animal has been hit in the centre of the paunch, chances are you will find very little blood, but there will be stomach contents in the area a few feet from the other side of where the animal was standing when you took the shot.

Finally, if the animal received only a minor flesh wound, you will find small drops of light-coloured blood along with hair fibres. Carefully examine the length and colour of the hair because this may give you clues on where the animal was hit.

To complicate matters, not all injuries result in an immediate or noticeable loss of blood. Case in point is if the animal was hit high in the chest below the spinal cord. That's why it is extremely important to take note of the animal's behaviour following the shot. In most cases, an animal will react in some way, perhaps staggering or jumping unnaturally. Even bristled hair can be evidence of a hit.

The first task if the animal has not dropped in its tracks is to precisely locate where the animal was standing at the moment of the shot. Next, mark the spot where you were standing when you took the shot by putting a glove or some other object up on a branch. The best material for this purpose is a strip of fluorescent surveyor tape. This way, if the recovery of the animal turns out to be difficult or if you have difficulty in finding the spot where the animal was standing, you can easily start over from the spot where you were standing. Once you locate a blood spoor, establish another marker with your fluorescent tape.

With that done, sit down and relax. Do not lurch off after the animal; rather wait the recommended period of time to allow the animal to bed down. Take the time to analyze the nature of the blood and try to establish where and how the animal was hit, taking into account its reaction at the time of the shot. Once the waiting time is over, move forward at little more than a creep, making as little noise as possible and carefully searching the surroundings. Sometimes an animal will double back, so it is important to be alert to every movement and shape. If it has not seen or heard you, chances are it will still be fairly close.

Photo 1.1 Small drops of light-coloured blood indicate that the moose was hit in the lungs.

Photo 1.2 A cow moose that fell in the water.

Photo 1.3 A rope tied around the antlers makes it easier to haul the animal up on shore.

Recovering an animal underwater

Sometimes a wounded animal will head for a body of water even when it has not been hit nearby. This can cause a number of problems. Certain measures for recovering the animal are more effective and safer, depending on whether it is male or female, submerged or floating, close to shore or farther out in deeper water.

More often than not, an animal which has died in the water will float (photo 1.2). Before trying to retrieve it, make sure that it is dead. Check the eyes; if they are open and

Recovering a submerged bull

Once the animal has been located underwater, use an anchor in an attempt to tangle a rope around the antlers.

unblinking, the game is safe to approach. Having an animal suddenly start to flail when you are next to it in a boat can have catastrophic results. Once you have determined it is safe to approach, you can set about towing the animal to shore. In the case of an antlered male, simply loop a rope around the headgear. If you have taken a female, run a rope around the neck or else cut a slit in the nose and pass the rope through it to tow the animal to shore.

Unfortunately, an animal may sink. Do not panic. You will probably still be able to recover it, but be careful not to roil the water which would impair visibility. The following techniques all require the use of a boat, a length of rope, an anchor and, of course, a safety vest (required by law in most regions of North America).

If you can see the animal, attach one end of the rope to the boat and the other end to the anchor. Now drop the anchor down close to the animal. If it is a female or a young animal with small antlers proceed in fairly wide circles around it with enough slack in the rope to snag around the legs. In the case of an antlered animal, make smaller circles and try to hook onto the tines as shown in the previous diagram.

Another method for recovering a submerged animal comes from native lore. You will need a long pole and a length of rope. Attach the rope firmly with a knot 12 to 18 inches (30 to 46 cm) from the end of the pole, then probe the bottom with the pole for the animal. Once you have positively located it, push the end of the pole into the mud close to the animal and make a circle around it by boat, keeping the rope as slack as possible. Once the rope is around the animal, gently raise both the pole and the rope, gradually pulling your game to the surface.

A winch or pulley makes hauling an animal out of a beaver pond relatively easy. Start by attaching one end of the pulley rope around the neck of the animal or the antlers. It is important to note that beaver ponds are often choked with dead trees and if you are trying to haul out a heavy-antlered bull moose, the antlers will constantly hang up in the branches. If chopping down some of these hurdles prove to be difficult, you may have to take the head off by severing the muscle at the base of the head. Now haul out the animal and the head separately.

Regular shooting practice is an essential preparation for your hunt and it determines your success. Spend enough time at the range and you will shoot with confidence. Combined with a detailed knowledge of the vital points of aim, it will guarantee that you will shoot accurately once the moment of truth arises.

And should the animal escape, remaining calm and in control will work to your advantage. The tracks left behind will be the unspoken clues that, if carefully analyzed, will tell you exactly what has transpired. These are the essential strategies of hunting and tracking and they will stand you in good stead.

Chapter 2

Too good to waste

Literally thousands of hunters head into the forests every year without the slightest idea of what to do after they have pulled the trigger and downed their game. The result of this ignorance is an enormous waste of delicious and irreplaceable venison each year. Let us quickly review some of the errors committed in the field and take a look at how they can be avoided.

Delayed field dressing

Without question, the most common reason for spoiled venison is waiting too long to dress the animal; that is, removing the entrails, cleaning the cavity and allowing the animal to cool. At its worst, this can result in a total loss of the animal.

Why? It is quite simple really. Even after the animal has died, the gastric juices continue to work, fluids ferment and because the heat can no longer be drawn away, this process actually accelerates. The heat produced by the fermentation process varies with the different species, but it prevents the essential cooling of the meat in all cases.

While the length of time before the meat is ruined varies, here is a rule of thumb. The maximum delay for caribou is approximately 30 minutes, for moose it is about two hours and three hours for deer. Of course, this will change to some degree with the outside temperature so that, on a warm day the process is accelerated and on a cold day it is slowed.

Nevertheless, if for reasons beyond your control, you have been unable to dress the animal within the guidelines stated above, there may still be hope of saving the meat. Immediately gut the animal and suspend it, even if the smell of rotten eggs from the carcass is strong. Once the carcass has been able to cool, check to see if the odour persists. If it is no longer noticeable, it means heating has only just started and you have managed to catch it in time. On the other hand, if the smell of rotten eggs persists, make a small incision in the rear quarter near the hip joint, reach in with a finger and probe around the back of the femur. If the smell on your finger is not strong, a good deal of the meat can still be saved. Otherwise, you will need to take the quarters to a qualified butcher or meat inspector for examination in order to determine whether any of the meat is useable.

Air circulation

A lack of adequate air circulation during the cooling process or while transporting the carcass can result in an enormous loss of meat.

After field dressing the animal, it is important to quickly cool the meat, regardless of whether the carcass is whole or in quarters. For the best cooling, it is better to suspend the animal right after cleaning it because this helps promote the circulation of air all around it (photo 2.1), accelerating the cooling process.

If that is not possible, raise the animal off the ground with small logs or stones so that the air can circulate under it. Regardless of whether the carcass is suspended or on the ground, it is essential to prop the flanks and chest cavity open with branches (photo 2.2) so that the heat can dissipate easily and quickly. In the case of a larger animal such as an elk or moose, it is best to cut the animal into quarters, but be sure to check on the regulations governing this in the area where you are hunting.

When you are transporting the carcass, smaller game such as deer can be placed on the roof of the vehicle, but contrary to the traditional positioning, it is important to place the chest cavity to the rear to ensure proper air flow. Transporting the animal in a trailer is ideal, provided the meat is protected from dust and sand. If you are transporting the quarters in a family sedan or van, take the time to protect the floor with a sheet of plastic or paper (photo 2.3). In addition, place several planks or blocks of wood under the quarters to keep the air circulating underneath them, thereby preventing the meat from heating (photo 2.4). Also, be sure to keep a window down, or the top back and the air vents fully open.

Some hunting lodges pack the quarters in special waxed meat boxes designed for air travel (photo 2.5). These boxes usually have holes in the sides to allow air circulation. They work fine for short periods of no more than a day in cool temperatures. Nevertheless, be sure to open the boxes as soon as you get home or to the butcher, because the meat will likely have heated to some degree during the trip. Another important point is to make sure that the meat has been properly cooled before placing it in any kind of closed container, including these meat boxes.

However, if the lodge prepares and cools or freezes the meat, you should leave the boxes closed until you are ready to place the meat into storage in order to avoid letting in heat.

Heat

Heat is meat's worst enemy. It can be a serious problem during the early seasons when the weather can swing from freezing to shirtsleeve temperatures over the course of just a few hours. For inexperienced hunters, these temperature swings can make the trip complicated and often results in some unpleasant surprises.

It is well understood that cooling is the only method of preserving meat without changing its flavour. The ideal temperature to store meat is between 34° and 37° F (1° to 3° C) with a level of humidity of 85%. That is the temperature you will find in the cool rooms of the best butcher shops.

The body temperature of a living deer, caribou, elk and moose is about 97.5° F (36.5° C). It takes between 15 and 18 hours for a carcass to reach the ideal storage temperature if weather conditions in the hunting area are favourable. If, however, the outside temperature is 60° F (15° C), the temperature of the meat will only drop to that level and there is serious danger of the meat spoiling (photo 2.6).

For all of these reasons, it is essential to cool the quarters as quickly as possible after field dressing the animal. One of the methods mentioned already is to hang the animal or quarters in a well ventilated, shaded area. The shorelines of lakes and rivers fit the bill particularly well and, as an added bonus, flies are less numerous there, making the job of caring

a)   b)

Photo 2.1 (a) In order to promote rapid cooling of the quarters with the skin on, it is essential to hang them in a shaded area and (b) cover them with cheesecloth.

Photo 2.2 Propping open the ribcage and abdomen with sticks helps the carcass cool quickly.

2.3   2.4

Photos 2.3 and 2.4 Here is the best way to keep your vehicle clean and, at the same time, ensure adequate air circulation around the quarters.

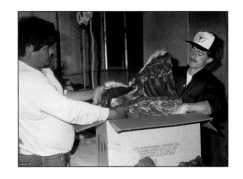

Photo 2.5 Waxed cardboard boxes intended for transporting meat should always have air vents.

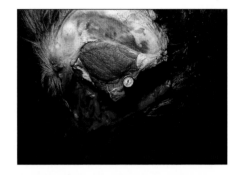

Photo 2.6 A thermometer inserted in the rear quarter of the animal (in this case a moose) indicated that the internal temperature has not yet dropped enough and after cooling is necessary.

Photo 2.7 Placing the quarters on shoreline boulders accelerates the cooling process.

for the meat less of a chore. If scavengers are not a concern, you can also put the animal or quarters on boulders or rocks at water level, provided you take lots of necessary precautions (photo 2.7).

If you are in a situation where a boat or canoe is available, place the quarters on blocks of wood, planks or even the oars in the boat and anchor it a distance out from the shore. Better yet, make a few turns of the lake with the boat with the meat on board. The air is usually several degrees cooler over the water and travelling with the meat on board circulates that air over the meat to cool it off faster. Furthermore, this circulation of cool air dries the membrane which covers the muscle tissue to create a parchment-like seal, making it difficult for flies to lay their eggs. While you are out on the water, you might also take advantage of the situation to clean off the quarters with a damp cloth; never pour water over the meat or immerse it in the lake.

Unfortunately, few hunters are aware of this method of cooling game. We have used it on many occasions and, based on its effectiveness, we highly recommend it. In fact, we have been able to come home with prime meat during early season hunts when other hunters who did not know to take advantage of the cooler lake air ran into problems with maggot infestations.

There are of course other techniques for cooling meat under these warm, calm early-season conditions, but none are as effective. That is why, when hunting moose, we field dress and quarter the animal as quickly as possible and then spend two to three hours travelling around on the lake with the meat. It is often the only way that we can prevent the loss of meat. In addition, if there are a lot of bluebottle flies on the gut pile (a sure sign of dangerously high temperatures) this is the best method available.

During periods of warm weather, bluebottle flies are a serious problem. Under no circumstances should you let these large, dark flies land on the meat because they will lay their eggs (photo 2.8) which transform into larvae (maggots) within 12 to 24 hours.

The flies have a tendency to lay their eggs in areas of clotted blood, particularly around severed veins and arteries through which the emerging maggots can access the meat. Carefully examine the vein which runs along the last rib (photo 2.9a), the femoral artery in the hind quarter (photo 2.9b) which runs along the backbone in the pelvic area, and check especially around the carotid artery in the neck. If the head has been removed, this latter location is particularly vulnerable. Also monitor the area of the bullet wound and make sure it has been carefully cleaned of all clotted blood.

If a few flies manage to lay their eggs despite your efforts, you might see a few maggots on the surface. If however, there are a lot of maggots on the meat, you will need to remove them and then trim a thin layer of meat away from the area. Now, make small incisions of about an inch (2.5 cm) deep along the blood vessel at intervals of about six inches (15 cm) until you find no more maggots in the vein or artery. They probably have not gone beyond that point.

Some hunters swear by the use of pepper to keep flies away, but the effectiveness of this method is difficult to prove. We have encountered some hunters who maintained that they were able to save their meat by abundantly covering the meat with cracked pepper, but in further discussions with them, we found that they also used several other time-tested methods, including cooling the quarters rapidly and wrapping them in cheesecloth. Therefore the question remains whether the pepper was actually necessary.

However, if you insist on using pepper to keep flies away from the meat, avoid putting more than a light dusting, and then only on the three major arteries as well as the area of the bullet wound. Pepper is a spice which will penetrate the meat and change its flavour. Save the spices for cooking!

Skin on, skin off

Many hunters skin their game in order to reduce weight for transport and weighing in at the butcher. However, this practice increases the loss of meat and reduces the quality. The skin is a natural protection, perfect for keeping the meat clean, flavourful and moist.

Commercial butchers who also process beef, veal and pork must, by law, remove the skin from hunted carcasses and keep them isolated from domestic carcasses. This is done to prevent the risk of cross-contamination.

Some retail butchers who offer game cutting have a separate cold room where only animals taken by hunting are stored. These butchers often allow you to hang the meat for aging with the skin on.

There are also businesses that only handle game. These will also often accept animals with the skin because they do not come in contact with domestic meat.

The cost for cutting the game is determined either by weight or a flat fee for the carcass. In the first instance, the animal is weighed and the figure is then multiplied by the base price charged per pound or per kilogram. If the animal is weighed with the skin on, you end up paying for the weight of the skin, which as well, pays for the skinning. In the second

Photo 2.8 An egg mass of maggots on a piece of meat.

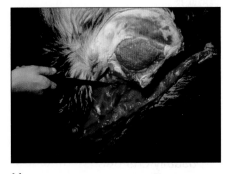

a)   b)

Photo 2.9 (a) The vein located near the middle of the first rib and (b) the femoral artery at the top of the filet near the coxal bone are areas where flies are most likely to lay their eggs.

Photo 2.10 The crust that developed on these skinned caribou quarters must be removed. This accounts for a substantial loss of meat.

Photo 2.11 It makes good sense to cover a deer with cheesecloth to protect it against flies, especially when the weather is warm.

case, a fixed amount is charged according to the size of the animal, small, medium and large. In this case, the butcher usually charges an additional fee for skinning the animal.

The crucial point to keep in mind here is that the meat is best when it is aged with the skin on, and the hunter needs to determine whether or not that is worth the extra cost. A moose aged with skin off for seven days forms a dark crust about a quarter inch (6 mm) thick, which then needs to be trimmed off. That represents a loss of seven or eight pounds (3.2 to 3.6 kg). Moose meat has been evaluated at $10 a pound ($22/kg) so that means a loss of $70 to $80 worth of prime venison. Compare that to the cost of leaving the skin on, about 50 pounds at 50 cents a pound (22.7 kg at $1.10/kg) or about $25.

On the hood

It is astounding to see hunters even today, who put their game on the hood of their car for transportation. The animal will absorb heat from the motor even over a short distance. It may well be a great place to show off your trophy, but we strongly recommend against it if you value your venison.

Questionable methods

One method we have encountered is to hang the quarters in a smoke hut in order to keep the flies off. The disadvantage of this practice is that the meat quickly picks up a smoky flavour and 200 pounds (90 kg) of smoked moose can grow tiresome to eat. In addition, your freezer will become impregnated with the smell.

The practice of attempting to cool the meat during hot weather by submerging it in plastic bags in a lake is a sure way to have it all go sour. First of all, you should never put uncooled meat in a sealed container or wrapping because if the heat cannot escape, the meat will start to rot very quickly. Furthermore, if the bag is not perfectly waterproof, water will seep in and be absorbed into the tissue. Not only will it make the meat look unpalatable, but the excess water will be released during cooking, resulting in the boiling rather than roasting of the meat. Waterlogged meat is also very difficult to preserve and, when frozen, the water will form ice crystals which will deteriorate the quality of the meat by breaking the muscle fibres. This will affect the texture and the flavour of the meat.

In conclusion, we would like to stress that the bigger the animal, the longer the cooling period, because the quarters are so much thicker. No matter what the size of the animal and the conditions under which it was taken, the secret to prime venison is quite basic: cool the meat as quickly as possible using the various methods that we have discussed previously. If you are lucky enough to have a boat at your disposal, do not hesitate to take advantage of this excellent method of cooling meat in remote areas.

Practical advice

Reasonable return

Most hunters leave the task of cutting the meat to a trained professional. Professional meat cutters have the expertise to get the most out of your hard-won game, however they are not magicians. The amount of meat you get from your game depends on how much care you have devoted to the carcass at each step.

For example, let us use a large animal like a bull moose that tips the scales at 1,185 pounds (537.5 kg) live and break it down into its components.

PORTIONS	POUNDS	KILOS	PERCENTAGE
Four quarters, skin off	700	317.5	59.1
Skin	75	34.0	6.3
Feet	50	22.7	4.2
Blood	60	27.2	5.1
Internal organs*	200	90.7	16.9
Head**	100	45.4	8.4
Total	1,185	537.5	100.0

- Starting with a live weight of 1,185 pounds (537.5 kg) you can expect a yield of between 33 and 35% of completely deboned meat. In other words, about 400 pounds (181.5 kg) of meat.

- If you know the weight of the four quarters with the skin on, you can calculate the yield of deboned meat at about 52%. Using that ratio, if your four quarters weigh 775 pounds (351.5 kg), you should end up with about 400 pounds (181.5 kg) of meat.

- When the quarters are weighed without the skin, you get a yield of about 57% of that amount.

- These ratios of yield are affected by the cleanliness of the carcass, the damage done by the bullet or bullets, whether the animal is aged with skin on or not and how long it is aged.

Deer

Deer are generally weighed as a complete carcass, with head, legs and skin included. Only the internal organs and the blood are removed. A hunter can usually expect to get roughly 50% of deboned meat from the field dressed animal. In other words, a deer that weighs 200 pounds (90 kg) field dressed should yield about 100 pounds (45.4 kg) of meat.

Here is another extrapolation. If the field-dressed carcass of a deer weighs 200 pounds (90 kg), the animal weighed about 260 pounds (118 kg) on the hoof. The intestines and respiratory system represent 50 pounds (22.7 kg) and the blood amounts to 10 pounds (4.5 kg). Together they represent about 23% of the live weight of the deer. So, to determine the live weight of a deer when you know the carcass weight of the field dressed deer, simply add 30% to the weight or multiply the known weight by a factor of 1.3.

These weights are approximate since many factors can affect the actual numbers.
* The internal organs are made up of the digestive system, the respiratory system and the edible organ meats.
** The weight of the head can vary according to the gender and age of the animal.

Chapter 3

The tenderness factor

The quality of the meat – specifically, the tenderness, flavour and texture – depends on a number of factors. There are the ante mortem conditions including the age of the animal before it was harvested, its daily habits and diet. In addition, heavy rutting activity as well as stress just prior to harvest will also play a role. There are also the post mortem conditions, specifically the degree of aging, which is directly related to the extent the carcass was cooled immediately after harvest. Whether it was kept properly cooled during transport to the butcher is another consideration.

Ante mortem conditions

Let us examine the moose situation. The meat of a six-month-old moose calf is extremely tender and the texture is so fine that it virtually melts in your mouth. That is because the animal has been nourished almost exclusively on tender vegetation and cow's milk.

At a year and a half, the meat of both the cows and bulls is almost as tender as that of calves in this second age category. The young bulls may well be in the midst of their first rut, but this has little effect on the tenderness of the meat.

The third age category includes moose between 2 ½ and 4 ½ years of age. Generally, the cows seek out and settle themselves into a relatively small area where food is plentiful and then move around only as much as necessary. Hence, they are able to gain substantial reserves of fat. The quality of meat from a barren or unbred female is exceptional. On the other hand, once a cow has calved once, the meat will have deteriorated somewhat because of the energy expended in feeding the calf. If the cow has raised twin calves, its meat will be less tender than if it had raised only a single calf.

Let us now take the case of a bull moose. During the September rut, a mature bull covers great distances in search of cows willing to breed and feeds just barely enough to keep from starving. In order to keep up the pace, it draws energy from its reserves, depleting the fat in and around the muscle tissue. The result is a deterioration of the quality and tenderness of the meat.

Younger bulls of 2 ½ years sport relatively small antlers and, because of this, rarely confront more mature and imposing bulls. On the other hand, 4 ½ years old males carry imposing headgear and will not often back down from a fight. That is why game butchers often find large bruises on the shoulders, flanks and thighs of big bulls inflicted by the antlers of their opponents. The meat of these animals can vary between moderately tender and slightly tough.

In the fourth age group, which includes moose between 5 ½ and 8 ½ years of age, you can encounter some unexpected surprises. For example, a lone bull roaming in a small area where cows are abundant will have meat which is moderately tender whereas a bull which has to do battle constantly to keep other bulls at bay will have very tough meat.

These prime and experienced bulls often have the largest antlers. They do not hesitate to confront other bulls, regardless of their size, and the battles they wage can be unbelievably violent. When the rivals are about the same size and of the same strength, the battles can be long and violent. In this case, even the usually tender cuts such as the backstraps and the filets are often as tough as shoe leather. If, however, one of the rivals is weaker, the battle is usually abandoned quickly and the quality of the meat is likely to be much better.

On the other hand, the meat of cow moose in this fourth age category is generally as tender as that of animals in the second group. Furthermore, it is rare to encounter a cow moose with meat that leaves anything to be desired.

Finally, the meat of old bulls is either tough or extremely tough and generally does not improve with aging. These animals are in their decline, yet they confront younger bulls in their prime, their urge to breed is still strong. The often one-sided battles against the stronger bulls seriously affect the quality of the meat.

In the case of the older females, the frequency of calving can be detrimental to the quality of the meat. A cow that has given birth every season throughout its life will have meat which is flabby and soft with a level of tenderness which leaves a lot to be desired. On the other hand, a cow which has been barren for several years will have much better meat because the animal will have been able to save its energy allowing the muscles to become strong and firm.

Deer & caribou

The aging process outlined for moose can also be used for deer and caribou. Spike bucks, usually a year and a half old, have a thick layer of fat and are generally quite tender. A doe which has given birth to one fawn is more tender than a female that has given birth to twin fawns. Furthermore, a buck harvested at the beginning of the rut will be somewhat more tender than a buck taken at the end of the rut.

At the same time, a deer that has matured in an area where food is abundant will have accumulated more surface and muscle tissue fat than one which has grown up in an area where browse is more difficult to obtain. Even if they are both the same age, the meat of the first will be more tender than the latter since the tenderness is directly related to the physical demands of the animal as well as the availability and quality of browse.

As far as caribou are concerned, there is a lesson to be learned from the habits of native hunters in the tundra. They will rarely if ever take a big, old bull during the autumn rut. That is because the meat of big bulls gives off an odour of urine when it is cooked. On the other hand, they do not hesitate to take a younger bull or cow.

In addition to the factors outlined above and included in the table on the following page, the state of stress at which the animal is in at the moment of harvest will influence the quality and tenderness of the meat.

41

Some animals give off an unpleasant odour of swamp and urine after being harvested. That is because males in full rut have an increased production of albumin. When this protein is present in the muscle tissues, it alters the colour and texture of the meat. No matter how much you season the meat, the flavour still persists and the liver of these animals is often yellowish or marbled. The odour is often encountered among cow moose as well because the female will roll in the urine of the bull just before being bred. However, it will not be found in the meat of the female because there is no albumin secretion.

Stress will also affect the quality of the meat, particularly if an animal has been wounded, chased or has just been involved in a battle with another male. The adrenaline secreted by the animal in response to the stress situation results in a build-up of lactic acid in the muscle tissues, raising the pH level of the meat. When this happens, the meat and blood tend to be very dark, with a sticky, pasty texture.

Post mortem conditions

Aging is a biochemical process which results in increased tenderness in all meats, including game. It is important to realize that very tough meat, such as that from an old bull will become only marginally more tender through aging while tender meat will benefit most from the process. The length of time the meat is aged determines how tender it becomes and this variable depends on how the carcass is cooled. These conditions, as we have discussed earlier, can be very different in the forest than in a butcher shop.

Under the ideal conditions found in a butcher shop with carefully controlled temperatures, a beef carcass requires about 12 hours to cool completely. The stiffness known as rigor mortis sets in between 12 and 24 hours after that and the aging process begins between the fifth and sixth day after the animal was harvested. It continues on average for between five and 12 days; it can be extended even longer but with an increasing loss of meat. The more meat is aged, the more tender it becomes but you also need to be aware that you will lose more of the animal in the trimming. Animals which have a good layer of fat to protect the meat and which were properly cleaned in the forest can be left to age as much as 15 days.

As a general rule, a big game animal can be aged for between five and 15 days, depending on the temperatures prevalent at the time it was harvested. The more time required for a carcass to cool, the shorter the aging period and conversely, the shorter the initial cooling time the longer the aging period possible. This is another reason to ensure that an animal is quickly cooled after being harvested.

Storage

Once you are out of the bush, it is important to get your big game animal into a butcher's cold room where the conditions are a stable 34° to 37° F (1° to 3° C) with a relative humidity of 85%.

A good way to test whether the animal has aged long enough is to press your thumb against the thin pleural membrane in the thorax and abdomen of the animal. If the imprint remains visible, the carcass has been aged enough and is ready to be cut. You should undertake this process the same day or, at the latest, the following day because, beyond that, you will lose more and more meat.

The following table outlines the approximate length of the aging period in a butcher's cold room, taking into account the three main factors previously discussed.

AGING PERIOD

Temperature at time of harvest	Cooling of the carcass	Circulation of air during transport	Recommended aging period
Cold 32° to 50° F (0° to 10° C)	12 to 15 hours	Very good	12 to 15 days
Mild 50° to 60° F (10° to 15.5° C)	15 to 18 hours	Good	10 to 12 days
Mild 50° to 60° F (10° to 15.5° C)	15 to 18 hours	Average	8 to 10 days
Mild 50° to 60° F (10° to 15.5° C)	15 to 18 hours	Poor	5 to 8 days
Warm 60° F or more (15.5° C or more)	18 to 24 hours	Poor	5 days

It is important to emphasize that the first choice lies with the hunter. It is up to you whether you are going for the battle-scarred trophy with a magnificent rack or, where the regulations permit, a less imposing young male or even female. The huge antlered male might make a great trophy on the wall, but gourmets will often opt to take an antlerless animal or even a young one. You need to decide whether you are hunting for antler or for meat.

Chapter 4

Tools & accessories

From saws to axes, sharpening stones to ropes, big game hunting requires the greatest array of equipment. The choice of models, makes and the quality of each is so enormous that it often becomes overwhelming.

To help you make the right choice, we have provided a detailed evaluation of the principal hunting tools and accessories in this chapter. In addition, we will discuss their use and care with some sharpening techniques.

Knives

The knife is, without question, the most important of all hunting tools (photos 4.1 and 4.2). To head into the forest without a proper knife is like hunting without the right calibre. When you are standing in front of the knife counter at a sporting goods store, avoid the pitfall of letting yourself be influenced by price or appearance. Bear in mind that a hunting knife can no more be pressed into doing double duty as a fish filleting knife any more than a fish filleting knife can be used to field dress big game. It is a real pity, but the knife that does it all has not yet been invented.

As can be seen in the following illustration, a knife is made up of three distinct elements – the blade, the guard (absent in the case of a folding knife), and the handle. Let us examine each of these characteristics individually in order to fully understand the make-up of a good hunting knife.

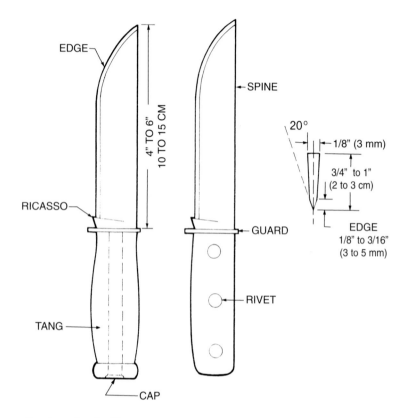

Parts of a knife

The blade

The three considerations to take into account in the search for a good blade are the composition of the metal, the size and the cutting edge.

Almost all knife blades are made from steel which is actually made by combining iron and carbon. After being mixed together in extremely hot furnaces, only between 1.1 and 4.0% carbon is left and this is the amount which determines the properties of the steel. Each knife maker has their particular trade secrets, adding varying amounts of tungsten, chromium, silicon, nickel and other elements in an effort to improve the blade in terms of lightness and strength. Stainless steel, made by adding nickel and chromium to the iron, is frequently used to make knives. The higher the chromium content of the steel, the more rust resistant the blade is.

Regardless of the composition of the blade, the steel must be tempered to harden it and make it somewhat bendable so it will not break easily. The hardness of the steel after tempering is expressed in units of Rockwell C. The harder the steel, the higher the Rockwell C value and conversely, the softer the steel, the lower the Rockwell C value.

A blade should fall between 52 and 56 on the Rockwell C scale. If the steel is tempered too high, the steel becomes harder, resulting in a fragile edge that tends to fracture when it comes in contact with a hard surface such as a bone. The steel is also too rigid and is difficult to sharpen. On the other hand, steel that is too soft will not hold its edge and will wear down quickly with each successive honing.

To sum up, a good hunting knife blade should be made from tempered steel with an average hardness (about 0.45% carbon content) and be stainless. Of course, it is impossible to tell the difference between soft steel and hard steel and the different levels of tempering when you are standing in front of a store's knife display. Nevertheless, refer to the manufacturers specifications either on the blade or in their brochure, even though only a few of them indicate the Rockwell C value.

Now let us go on to the second aspect, the size of the blade.

A hunting knife should have a spine of no more than ⅛ inch (3 mm). If a blade is too thick, it tends to be unnecessarily heavy. Furthermore, as the years go by and the blade is repeatedly honed, it tends to become more and more difficult to sharpen. The problem is that each honing takes away a minute amount of steel and, after honing the knife several hundred times, the edge creeps closer and closer to the heavy spine, forcing the angle of the edge to become more obtuse.

The spine of the blade should ideally be straight. A trailing point style in which the tip rises higher than the spine should be avoided since it tends to be a problem during field dressing. It is also dangerous. A large point is best suited for skinning rather than field dressing. The curve of the point need not be too pronounced; an arc of 1 ¼ to 1 ½ inches (3 to 4 cm) from the point is sufficient.

Ideally, the blade should be between ¾ and 1 ¼ inch (2 to 3 cm) wide. If it is wider than that, it can become cumbersome during the gutting. Also when you are boning out the meat, it will not easily slip between the bones.

In terms of length, look for a blade four to six inches long (10 to 15 cm). A longer blade tends to be heavier and you risk puncturing the paunch.

Now let us take a look at the edge of the blade. When it was manufactured, the knife had no edge at all and the subsequent ¨V¨ shape of the edge is created by honing. When a knife becomes dull, it is because the point of the ¨V¨ is increasingly rounded.

It is critical that each side of the ¨V¨ is exactly the same height – between ⅛ and 3/16 inch (3 to 5 mm) – and that the angle formed is between 15 and 20 degrees.

An edge with too great an acute angle will be too fragile and will chip easily, requiring frequent honing. On the other hand, if the angle is too open (obtuse), it will not have enough edge to easily cut through the hide or meat of the animal.

The guard

The guard is a safety measure which prevents the fingers from sliding forward off the handle and onto the blade. The configurations differ from one model to another, but the important thing, if you value your fingers, is that the knife has some sort of guard.

The handle

The handle of a knife can be made in many different shapes and a variety of materials including wood, bone, antler, leather and synthetic materials. The choice depends entirely on what you find pleasing. The only factors you need to consider are how the handle is attached to the blade and how comfortably it fits into your hand.

Check to make sure that the handle is firmly attached to the tang (the steel extension of the blade into the handle). Knife manufacturers use two primary methods (occasionally a combination of the two) to attach the handle. Both are equally good. One method is to use a full tang. This means that the steel has the same outline as the handle, and the handle components (called scales in this case) are attached with two or preferably three rivets. The other method uses a through tang. In this case the part of the steel which extends into the handle is narrow and not visible. It extends through a channel in the handle material to protrude at the metal end cap where it is either held with a screw nut or permanently attached. A partial tang uses a combination of both, in that the steel extends only about half-way up into the handle and is held into place with a rivet.

Regardless of which style of handle you prefer, the way it feels in your hand is critical. Your hand should fit completely around it to ensure a firm grip. Also ensure that the knife cannot rotate in your hand.

Sheath

A sheath needs to be both utilitarian and safe. It should also be made of good, strong cowhide that is easy to maintain. The stitching should be located so that the keen edge of the blade does not come in contact with it. Rivets are frequently used for reinforcement. A quality sheath will have an extra layer of leather (called a welt) added between the panels before they are stitched together in order to hold the knife properly.

The sheath should also have a solid tab with a snap or a leather thong to hold the knife in place and prevent it from slipping out. Check the belt loop. The manufacturer will have used either two incisions in the back of the sheath at the handle or else a loop of the sheath leather itself. In either case, remember that hunting belts are generally wider and thicker than dress belts, so make sure the sheath will accommodate the style of belt you will be wearing.

Another style of knife is the folder (photo 4.3). Most of the criteria outlined for the fixed blade knives also apply to the folder. Some excellent models are available. The blade is generally shorter, measuring 3 to 4 ½ inches (8 to 11 cm). Some hunters prefer this compact format. The fact that the sheath completely encases the knife when not in use is another advantage. Some models even have blades which can be removed, making it easier to clean and maintain the knife.

If you do opt for a folding knife, insist on a locking model which prevents the blade from accidentally closing. Also make sure the blade does not bottom out in its groove when the knife is closed. This prevents it from becoming blunt.

Photo 4.1 Here are a few different models of excellent knives from different manufacturers. From left to right: Browning, Katar, Savana, Buck and Browning.

Photo 4.2 Some more quality knives. Two boning knives made by Giesser, the first with a wood handle and the second with a synthetic handle; a Puma with a saw edge on the spine; a DS knife with a pronounced guard; a Savana with a slight trailing point; a Buck hunting knife and a Buck skinner.

Photo 4.3 Here are some folding knives. From top to bottom: a Browning folder with one blade, a Browning folder with three blades (saw, regular blade and gutting blade), a Puma and two Wyoming knives, the first with plastic scales and the second with metal scales.

Photo 4.4 Gutting knives. The two upper models have auxiliary blades, one with a protective shield and the other without. The lower model has no auxiliary blade.

Photo 4.5 Different sharpening systems. At the left are Choc Stick ceramic rods with a wooden case; natural whetstones in medium and fine grit by Smith; natural stone in fine grit on a wooden base as well as a set of three stones and oil on a wooden base both made by Washita; two artificial stones with dual grits (the one on the right is offered by Browning); and a set of two stones and oil in a case by Smith.

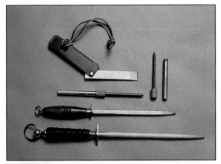

Photo 4.6 From top to bottom: a sharpening steel made by Gerber; collapsible sharpening steels by EZE-LAP (one assembled the other unassembled); a small kitchen sharpening steel and a butcher's steel.

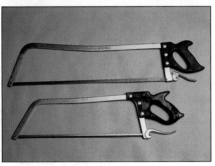

Photo 4.7 Butcher saws. The smaller one at the bottom is more practical for transportation.

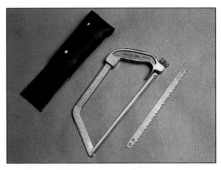

Photo 4.8 A Wyoming saw with interchangeable blades, along with the sheath.

Photo 4.9 A all-purpose saw made by Pioneer, along with its sheath.

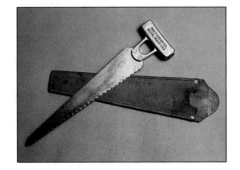

Another style is the gutting knife (photo 4.4) which, as the name implies, is a specialized tool used for gutting an animal. Remember that you will still need another knife to quarter your game. The advantage is that the shape of the gut hook substantially reduces the risk of perforating the intestines during evisceration. Two models are available: with or without an auxiliary extension blade. The extension blade is extremely sharp and is used only to cut through the skin and around the anus. The extension is protected with a plastic cover when not in use to prevent injury. The knife comes with a sheath that covers it completely. The blades are of excellent quality and are removable.

In closing, let us examine the costs of a good hunting knife.

You do not need to spend a year's salary as there is a wide choice of excellent fixed-blade models within $40 to $100 range. For a good folding knife, plan on paying between $50 and $90, although if you opt for models with interchangeable blades, you will need to spend about $100. Gutting knives sell for approximately $40.

However, if none of the over-the-counter knives meet your needs and requirements, or if you just prefer to have something unique, you can have a knife-maker custom design a knife to your specifications. The choice of material and shape is limited only by your imagination, but you should plan on paying three to four times as much as a production model.

Sharpening stones

Regardless of whether you own several knives or have just bought your first one, remember that the edge will not stay razor sharp forever. Sooner or later, it will need to be sharpened. Furthermore, no conscientious hunter will venture afield without carefully checking over all his equipment. This includes making sure that the knife is properly sharpened. So let us review some of the products offered for that purpose.

There is no question that a sharpening stone (photo 4.5) is the best tool to restore the edge on any knife. Stores which sell hunting and fishing equipment, cutlery shops and a variety of other knife vendors usually offer sharpening stones in different shapes, textures and quality.

Remember, whether you prefer an oil stone or water stone, there are essentially two different kinds, natural and artificial.

Natural stones are extracted from the ground. One of the sources is the state of Arkansas and neighbouring areas. Hence the name Arkansas stone. The advantages of this product are their superior quality and reasonable price. The disadvantage is that natural stones break easily.

Artificial stones are industrially produced. They consist of carbon, aluminium and other similar elements. The advantage of artificial stones is that they are available in a variety of textures and abrasions. Furthermore, it is possible to have different grits imbedded on the two faces of the same stone.

All stones are categorized according to their grit, similar to sandpaper, except that the grades are not listed numerically but rather by the degree of cutting power: rough, medium, fine and extra-fine. Generally natural stones are available in medium, fine and extra-fine grades while artificial stones are usually rough, medium or fine.

Each of the grades or textures has its particular purpose. A rough texture is used solely when the edge of a blade is extremely dull. Medium grain is used to grind an edge which has been rounded through use. Once the edge has been restored or a blade needs only a light touch-up, the fine grain is the best stone to use. Extra fine grain stones are used to polish the edge for an ultra-keen blade.

The truth is that you really only need two stones, a medium and a fine grain. Rather than buying two stones, consider an artificial stone with two grits, a medium on one face and a fine on the other. For home or cabin use, stones six to eight inches (15 to 20 cm) in length and 2 ¼ to four inches (6 to 10 cm) wide are ideal. However, for use in the field, a smaller stone measuring three to four inches (8 to 10 cm) long and two inches (5 cm) wide is more practical since it is lighter and more compact.

Another useful item is a small sharpening steel (photo 4.6) made from a length of metal or ceramic. Some models can be taken apart, making them even more compact. You have probably seen a butcher use a larger version of a sharpening steel, repeatedly running the blade along the length of the steel, alternating from one side to the other. Sharpening steels are used only to maintain an edge, not to restore a blade which has become dull through extensive use.

An important point to remember regarding knife sharpening is to never use a stone without first giving it a coat of liquid: oil for an oil stone, or water for a water stone. Coating the stone prevents undue friction of metal against the grit and it also floats the steel particles to the surface, preventing them from clogging the grit. Special oils are available to improve the cutting properties of the stone, but if you are in the middle of the bush, just plain water will do the trick.

In order to prevent the stone from sliding around during use, place it on a flat, rough surface or on a wet rag. This will reduce the risk of annoying accidents. If the stone comes in a fitted box, place the damp rag under the wooden box to hold it in place.

Once you have finished, check the edge by running your thumb lightly across it; the ridges of your skin should catch on the edge rather than slide smoothly across it. If you are having trouble getting a keen edge, the problem might be that you are having difficulty keeping the edge constant. In

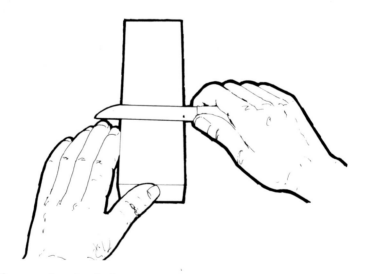

Sharpening techniques
a) Place the edge of the blade on the stone so that it forms an angle of between 15 and 20 degrees with the ricasso (the short section of the blade immediately in front of the guard) close to the stone.

b) Slide the blade across the stone so that the entire edge comes in contact with the grit, as if you were trying to slice a thin sheet off the stone.

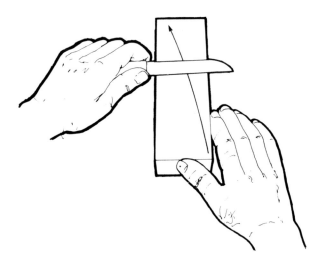

c) To hone the other side of the blade, proceed as in step b, but hold the knife in your other hand. Be sure to keep the angle consistent at 15 to 20 degrees and run the knife across the stone the same number of times on both sides.

this case, pick up a sharpening system which clamps the blade firmly in place at a constant angle to the stone.

Axes

Many hunters swear by their axes. In fact, this tool is indispensable to anybody who plans to venture into the forest because it has a wide variety of uses. For the big game hunter, especially the moose hunter, it is an important piece of equipment because it can be used to cut down along the backbone, making it easy to quarter the otherwise unmanageable carcass of such a large animal. This technique is explained in greater detail in Chapter 6.

While we are on the subject, it is sad to see that the majority of hunters who make use of axes do not understand the basics. One wrong move can ruin several pounds of meat, so it is important to take your time when using one.

A small, portable axe that can be carried on the belt is most practical. Ideally, it should have a total length of no more than 20 inches (50 cm) and the handle should be made from hardwood (maple or oak) shaped along the grain of the wood.

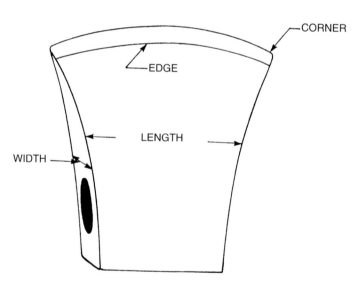

The axe head

The head of an axe used for hunting should not weigh more than three pounds (1.5 kg). The back of the head should be flat and slightly shorter than the blade. The blade itself should form the arc of a circle over its entire length and, for safety reasons, the corners should be slightly rounded.

The end of the handle should be wide enough to provide a solid grip. (The characteristics of the head of the axe are described in the caption of the previous diagram.)

The technique used to sharpen an axe is outlined below. It requires a vice or clamps and a flat file. Before starting, make sure that the head of the axe is firmly held in the vice.

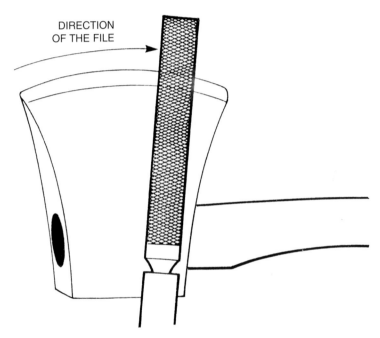

DIRECTION OF THE FILE

Axe sharpening technique
Standing in front of the vice, run the file smoothly across the edge of the axe, as indicated in the diagram, applying even pressure. A ¼ inch (6 mm) edge is plenty.

In the bush, a medium grit stone is sufficient to repair any damage or to simply maintain the edge when necessary.

Prior to your departure, make sure the axe head is firmly attached to the handle. If not, remove the protective case and submerge the head and part of the handle in a container of water to make the wood swell. Now replace the wedge with one slightly bigger than the original, using either wood or metal. Next, coat the head of the axe with linseed oil or animal grease to protect it against rust. Finally, examine the case to make sure it is in good shape.

Saws

There is nothing better than a good saw to do a clean job of dressing game in the bush. The thin blade and fine teeth make it possible to run a clean cut with no splinters, ultimately providing a better return on the meat.

Without question, the best model is a butcher's saw (photo 4.7). These have become so popular among hunters that several manufacturers have introduced compact saws aimed at this market. They are available at both butcher supply stores and sporting goods stores.

This saw has a 21-inch (53 cm) blade compared to the 26- inch (66 cm) model used by butchers. It is a rule of thumb that the longer the blade, the easier the task. The saw should also have a quality metal frame and the plastic handle should be comfortable in the hand.

Several manufacturers, including Wyoming, offer saws with interchangeable blades (photo 4.8), including one with coarse teeth for sawing wood and another with smaller teeth for cutting through bones. The frame comes in three pieces and the blades are about 10 inches (25 cm) long. The total saw length is 13 inches (33 cm) when assembled, yet it can be taken apart and placed in a case which can be carried on your belt.

You can also opt for an all-purpose saw (photo 4.9) which boasts a fixed blade with fine teeth on one side and coarser teeth on the other. With a metal grip, this saw is offered in two sizes – 10 and 15 inches (25 and 38 cm) – and also comes in a leather case that can be carried on a belt.

Ropes

No hunter should head afield without some rope in the packsack.

For moose hunting, a 60-foot (18 m) length of rope with at least 1,000 pounds (450 kg) of strength will solve a lot of problems. A second smaller rope 50 feet (15 m) long and with a strength of 250 pound (115 kg) test will come in handy to hold the animal in place for field dressing, to suspend the quarters or to build a shelter. For deer hunting, the latter is plenty.

Hemp ropes are the best, but they tend to be expensive. Woven cotton ropes (see following diagram) are somewhat less expensive and still quite good. Yellow nylon ropes with three or four strands tend to be rather stiff and are better suited to water sports.

Cotton Rope
Most cotton ropes are made up of a central core covered with a woven sheath. The more it is pulled the stronger it becomes.

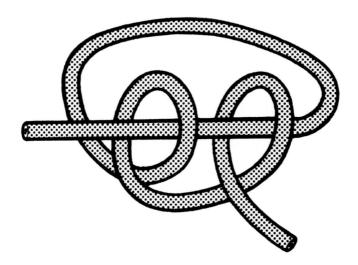

Double knot
The double knot is used to keep the ends from unravelling.

Before using a rope, it is important to sear the ends and lock them with a double knot to keep them from unravelling. Rope which has been soiled with blood can be washed by soaking it overnight in cold water and detergent. The next day, simply rinse out the rope and hang it up to dry.

59

In some cases, a hoist can come in handy. Models made from metal are cumbersome to carry around, but for those who hunt from boats or close to a camp or vehicle, they are just great. Hoists capable of handling up to 2,000 pounds (900 kg) with about 20 feet (6 m) of steel cable are ideal. To double the capability of the hoist, you will need to double the cable.

However, a model with a cotton rope capable of holding 1,100 pounds (500 kg) and four or six pulleys is even easier to use. Wear gloves to get a better grip on the rope. Keep in mind that cotton rope tends to stretch and can only be used effectively on smaller animals.

Cheesecloth bags

Cheesecloth bags (photo 4.10) are indispensable for big game hunting. They can be used to keep flies off the meat and keep it clean during transportation, thereby minimizing the unnecessary loss of venison.

Cheesecloth is used primarily to cover the carcass, whole or in quarters, while it is being cooled as well as during the aging process. Since it allows the circulation of air, the process is in no way compromised. The meat is also protected against flies trying to lay their eggs on the meat as well as against dust, soil, twigs and leaves. Finally, cheesecloth can be used as straps to carry the quarters or as rags to clean the carcass, which is particularly useful if you have perforated an intestine.

There are several different types of cheesecloth available; the type that comes sewn together along one side is more useful than the one that comes open. It is usually sold in bags of about a pound (450 g) or more.

Cheesecloth is reusable. Just let it soak overnight in soapy, cold water and wash it the next day. Dry it in a dryer if you have one readily available.

Some hunters prefer to cover the quarters with sheets held in place with clothespins or cords. It is a good option provided the sheet permits the circulation of air so that the meat can cool properly.

Burlap used over a layer of cheesecloth provides greater strength during transportation. Burlap bags with cord closures (photo 4.11) are available and they are large enough to cover a whole rear quarter of a moose.

Peach paper

Used extensively by butchers, peach paper allows air to pass through and at the same time prevents the meat from becoming dark (can be replace by scale paper).

It can be extremely useful for a variety of purposes, including separating cuts of meat, providing a clean area to place cuts for cooling and even to temporarily close accidental cuts in the intestines. Ask your butcher for a few sheets before you head out on your next big game hunting trip.

Rain pants

Field dressing a large animal such as a moose can be dirty work. To avoid unnecessarily getting your clothes full of blood and dirt, simply slip on a pair of rain pants. Once you are done, all you have to do is rinse them off at the first available source of water. They are light and hardly take up any room. The only disadvantage that I have come across is that in the excitement of it all, I sometimes forget to put them on until it is too late.

Gloves

Moose, elk, caribou and deer are susceptible to a variety of diseases, including tuberculosis and so it is a good idea to wear gloves while field dressing the animal. Surgeon's gloves are ideal because they are extremely light and thin. They conform to the shape of the hand and feel as if you are not wearing them at all. You can also wear rubber gloves such as those used for doing dishes. Since they are longer they will protect your forearms to some extent. Chose the thinnest available.

Whether or not you are in the habit of carrying a pair of gloves, it is the wise thing to do, particularly if you have some kind of injury, burn or skin irritation.

While on the subject, make sure you always have a first aid kit on hand and meticulously disinfect any cut incurred while handling the meat, no matter how small.

Others

In addition to a small first aid kit and survival kit, always carry a flashlight in your back pack. It will come in handy if

Photo 4.10 Cheesecloth bags.

Photo 4.11 Burlap bag with draw-string.

Photo 4.12 Peach paper and ther-mometer.

you need to clean an animal after dark. However, be sure to check the regulations governing the use of flashlights while hunting in your area.

HUNTING CHECK LIST

Moose, elk & caribou hunting

- 1 knife
- 1 sharpening stone or steel
- 1 saw or axe
- 1 rope with 1,000 pound (450 kg) test strength for moose or 300 pounds (135 kg) for caribou
- 1 rope with 250 pound (115 kg) test strength
- 1 or 2 large cheesecloth bags
- Peach paper
- 1 pair of rain pants
- Surgical gloves
- Flashlight

Deer hunting

- 1 knife
- 1 sharpening stone or steel
- 1 saw or axe
- 1 rope with 250 pound (115 kg) test strength
- 1 cheesecloth bag
- Peach paper
- 1 pair of rain pants
- Surgical gloves
- Flashlight

Now you are properly equipped and ready to go. It is also very important that your equipment is in good shape. Even quality tools become ineffective and dangerous if they are not properly maintained.

Chapter 5

Field dressing

Once you have pulled the trigger, the fun is over and the work begins. Fortunately, it is not nearly as complicated and difficult as it appears. The task boils down to a series of logical steps with well-defined reference points and before you know it, you are finished. Field dressing a moose, the largest of our North American big game animals, should take no more than about 30 minutes. First, however let us discuss the question of bleeding a game animal.

Bleeding

The myth that all game needs to be bled probably started many years ago with farmers who butchered their own meat. At that time and even in the modern abattoirs of today, it was a matter of necessity. The animal is first rendered unconscious which means that it is still breathing and its blood is still circulating. In this unconscious state, when the animal is bled, the heart is still pumping, and virtually all of the blood is drained from the body.

Therein lies the difference between an animal which is slaughtered in an abattoir and one which is slain by a hunter in the field. In the abattoir, an animal's heart must still be able to pump the blood while a hunter aims for the vital target on an animal and, when successful, the heart stops beating. Once hit, the heart ceases pumping blood, so very little is accomplished by cutting the throat of the animal. All that the hunter accomplishes is to empty some of the blood from the artery which runs from the heart to the head. Nothing more. Furthermore, the blood which drains into the chest of the animal is emptied out during the field dressing and by the action of pumping the limbs. The animal is essentially being bled from the moment the bullet or arrow passes through it; the only difference is that the bleeding occurs internally.

On the other hand, if an animal has been hit in the spinal column and is either partially or completely paralyzed, it is still conscious to some degree. Rather than rushing in and trying to bleed the animal and, in the process risking serious injury to yourself, the proper thing to do is to dispatch it with a follow up shot as quickly as possible. Aside from the moral issues, the problem with trying to bleed the animal is that it undergoes severe stress that in turn will result in a poor quality meat.

Some hunters maintain that if you do not bleed the animal, it will have a bad taste. Do not buy into this theory. Bleeding takes place automatically during evisceration.

Another problem with trying to bleed an animal by cutting its throat is that it results in irreparable damage to the cape. If you were planning to have the head or whole animal mounted, it is best to avoid cutting the throat. The damage done to the pelt will result in a poor quality mount at best, and at worst renders the cape unusuable.

Prior to field dressing

When you approach game which has been downed, it is essential to do so cautiously since it may still be alive, and active enough to cause serious injury. Always walk up from behind watching carefully for any sign of movement. The two best indicators are the eyes and the tongue (photo 5.1). If the eyes are open, and the tongue is hanging the animal has given up its soul, if not you need to finish the job as quickly as possible. In the case of a female, aim for the ear in order to penetrate the brain. With males with antlers you want to keep, a bullet in the nape of the neck will accomplish the same thing. The two different methods result in minimal loss of meat. Make sure, however, that the shots are safe and that there is no one either in front or beyond the animal and that there is nothing in the way to deflect the shot.

Once the animal is dispatched, it is time to get to work. The first task is to attach the permit stubs or tags (photo 5.2) as required by the game regulations in the area you are hunting. The next step is to place the animal in a position

Photo 5.1 A dead animal has open eyes and a hanging tongue.

Photo 5.2 Where required by law, game tag should be attached to the animal as soon as it is recovered.

appropriate for field dressing, in other words, on its back. The antlers of a male help tremendously by holding the animal in place. In the case of a female, attach the front legs to some nearby trees and then place logs or stones under the shoulders to raise them slightly.

The organ meats

It is a good idea to remove the organ meats (heart, liver, kidneys) as you get to them so you do not forget them later.

These organs will cool much faster if you place them on a sheet of peach paper or scale paper (photo 5.3) or any other clean piece of paper. If possible, suspend the heart and liver from a branch using the rubbery vessels that run through them. Once they have cooled, it is a good idea to cover them

Photo 5.3 In order to keep the organ meats clean, place them on clean paper, peach paper or in a container as soon as they are removed.

Photo 5.4 A length of cheesecloth knotted at both ends is ideal for transporting the organ meats.

with cheesecloth bags to protect them from flies. It also makes them easier to carry (photo 5.4). The removal of the tongue and brain, along with the proper preparation of organ meats, is discussed in Chapter 7.

Steps to follow

The explanatory captions which accompany the following illustrations provide complete information on the field dressing of all game animals while those photos which have numbers in brackets apply to caribou. The techniques shown here are applicable to all members of the deer family as well as mountain sheep, goats and pronghorn antelope.

Releasing the anus

In releasing the anus (photos 5.5 and 5.6), do not worry about damaging any meat since there is little in this area other than pelvic bone. Do not forget to tie the anus closed using a piece of string to prevent fecal mater from soiling the meat (photo 5.7).

In the case of a female, remove the vulva and anus in one single operation. Check to see if the female is lactating by pulling on the teat while squeezing it. This information is useful to game biologists and, the absence of milk in the case of an older barren cow is an indication of the tenderness of the meat.

When you remove the penis of the male (photos 5.8), avoid spilling urine on the meat.

Cutting the skin

For the next step, cutting the skin on the sternum (photo 5.9), you need to decide whether you intend to have the head mounted. If you do not plan to take the cape, start the incision at the base of the lower jaw and continue right to the front of the sternum near the neck. If you plan to have the head mounted and want to take the cape, you will need to start the incision behind the sternum (see also Chapter 10).

The next step is to cut open the skin on the abdomen (photo 5.11). This can be done one of several ways as shown in the illustrations on the opposite page. You can first cut the skin and then the membrane which covers the paunch or, in

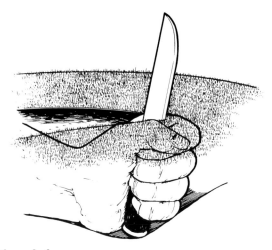

Cutting the abdomen

Method A – Insert the handle of the knife into the abdomen at the sternum leaving the tip extended outside the animal. Then cut the skin, holding the knife firmly.

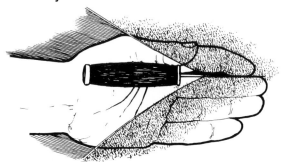

Method B – Insert your hand or place two fingers into the paunch at the sternum and hold the blade edge up between them. Cut the skin while guiding the blade away from the intestines and other organs.

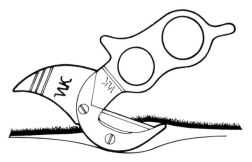

Method C – Using a gut hook makes it easier to cut the skin and membrane covering the paunch.

BONE STRUTURE OF A CARIBOU

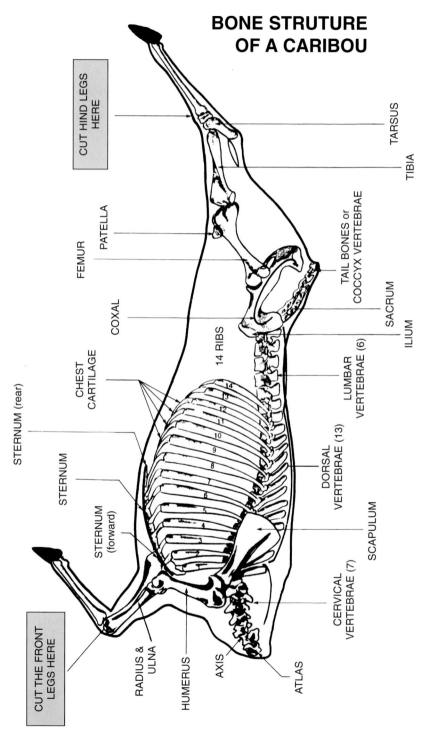

CUT HIND LEGS HERE

TARSUS

TIBIA

PATELLA

FEMUR

TAIL BONES or COCCYX VERTEBRAE

SACRUM

ILIUM

COXAL

14 RIBS

CHEST CARTILAGE

STERNUM (rear)

STERNUM

LUMBAR VERTEBRAE (6)

DORSAL VERTEBRAE (13)

STERNUM (forward)

SCAPULUM

RADIUS & ULNA

HUMERUS

AXIS

CERVICAL VERTEBRAE (7)

ATLAS

CUT THE FRONT LEGS HERE

70

BONE STRUTURE OF A DEER

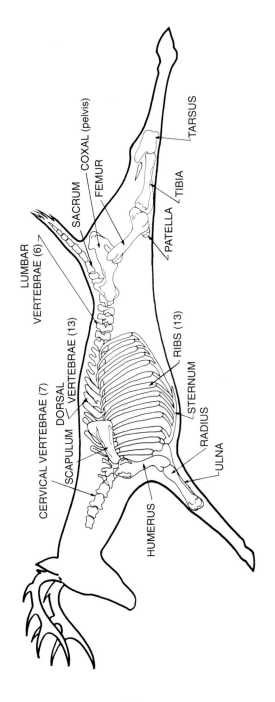

BONE STRUTURE OF A MOOSE

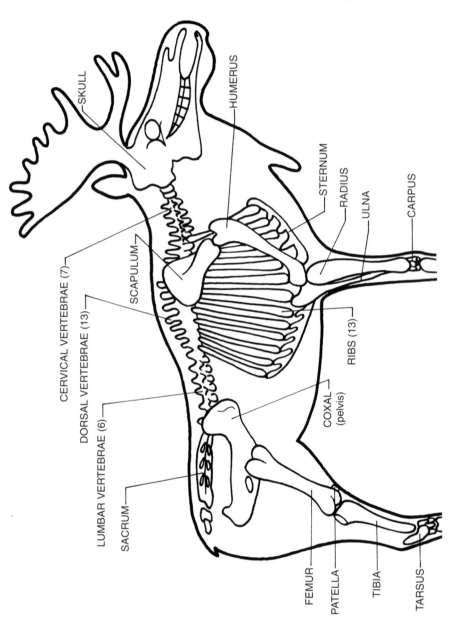

order to save time, cut both together at the same time using a knife (illustrations A & B) or gutting hook (illustration C). In either case, it is important to avoid perforating any of the organs in the paunch area.

Cutting the sternum

You can cut the sternum (photo 5.10) either prior to or subsequent to the previous step.

Removing the paunch

The internal organs are removed starting from top to bottom in the following order: first the heart, then the oesophagus, windpipe and lungs. Tie off the oesophagus and windpipe to prevent stomach contents from trickling out. Then cut the diaphragm which is the flat fold of thin muscle separating the latter organs from the liver and intestines.

After you have cut the ligaments which support the intestines remove them from the cavity. Since they give off a fair amount of heat, it is a good idea to drag them about a dozen feet (four meters) to the side so that the carcass can cool faster. Photos 5.12 to 5.29 clearly illustrate the steps that need to be followed.

Pumping

Pumping the muscle tissues (photo 5.30) in order to compress them squeezes out the remaining blood. In order to accomplish this, flex the front and rear legs repeatedly until

CARIBOU

Photo 5.5 Using the point of your knife, cut around the anus, between ½ to ¾ inch (1 to 2 cm) back.

Photo 5.6 Pull on the anus until you have been able to withdraw 4 to 5 inches (10 to12 cm) of large intestine.

73

Photo 5.7 Tie off the large intestine.

a)   b)

Photo 5.8 In order to remove the testicles and penis, (a) make a cut on either side of the penis (about the diameter of a pencil) right to the rectum and then (b) cut it off.

Photo 5.9 Cut the skin from the neck to the end of the sternum.

Photo 5.10 Open the sternum lengthwise using a saw.

74

a)

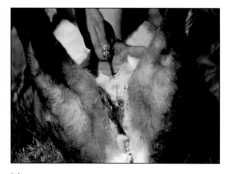

b)

Photo 5.11 Cut the hide along the belly starting from the sternum and ending at the anus, using either (a) a gutting knife or (b) a regular hunting knife.

Photo 5.12 Slice through the membrane that surrounds the heart.

Photo 5.13 Remove the heart by pulling it toward you and cutting the arteries that are attached to it.

Photo 5.14 The heart once it has been taken out.

Photo 5.15 Cut along the oesophagus, separating it from the ligaments which hold it against the meat.

Photo 5.16 Tie off the extremity of the oesophagus with a piece of string.

a)   b)

Photo 5.17 (a) Cut the ligaments that hold the oesophagus and (b) remove it gradually by pulling gently toward the back of the animal.

Photo 5.18 The lungs are the next organs to come out.

Photo 5.19 Once the lungs are removed, you can work on the liver.

a)

b)

Photo 5.20 But first, you need to remove one of the kidneys (a). It is located at the thickest part of the liver and (b) can be removed by pulling it gently away.

Photo 5.21 Now remove the liver.

Photo 5.22 Scratch the surface of the liver with the blade of your knife.

Photo 5.23 With the liver out of the way, you can now remove the second kidney.

Photo 5.24 Remove the membrane which covers the kidneys.

Photo 5.25 Cut the muscle tissues between the two hind legs right down to the pelvis.

Photo 5.26 Using a knife or saw, cut the pelvis between the two legs.

Photo 5.27 Pull the large intestine loose.

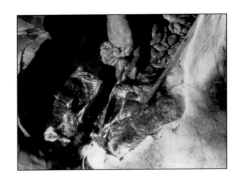

Photo 5.28 Remove the entrails from the cavity of the animal.

Photo 5.29 The hardest part of the work is over.

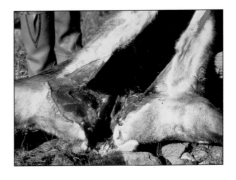

Photo 5.30 Pump the animal by flexing the hind and the front legs several times to remove as much blood as possible.

no more blood flows. It may seem like a lot of trouble, but it reduces the amount of blood that seeps out during transportation.

Sternum

Almost all game animals are field dressed in this manner except for smaller game such as deer and antelope. In the latter cases, most hunters do not split the sternum open in the field. They simply detach the anus and then open the paunch to remove the entrails. However, they encounter some difficulty in removing the heart and lungs because the interior of the chest is a fairly restrained area.

The sternum can be cut with a strong knife. After having cut the skin which covers the chest, cut through the small cartilages (eight on each side) which hold the sides together. Once this is done, spread the chest cage apart and use a small stick to hold it open. You can also use a saw to split the chest open by cutting down the center of the sternum.

DEER

Photo 5.31 It is been a hard hunt, but you have taken your deer.

Photo 5.32 Since deer are comparatively small, they can be held steady in this position.

In addition to making the job of cleaning out the animal easier, splitting the chest also promotes quicker cooling.

a)

b)

Photo 5.33 Cut around the anus with the point of your knife (a & b).

Photo 5.34 Cut the ligaments attached to the large intestine.

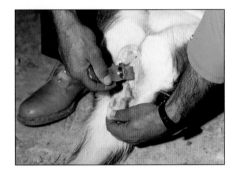

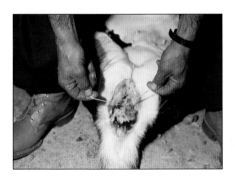

Photo 5.35 Tie off the anus.

Photo 5.36 Grab a piece of the hide at the belly and make a small incision.

a)   b)

Photo 5.37 (a) Insert two fingers in the opening and (b) placing your knife between them cut the skin right down to the anus.

 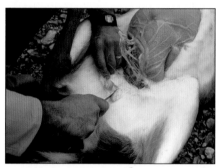

Photo 5.38 Position your two legs so that the hind legs of the deer are spread open.

Photo 5.39 Cut the skin of the scrotum and remove the testicles.

a)   b)

Photo 5.40 In order to remove the penis, (a) first make an incision, then (b) remove it by pulling on it and (c) cutting it at the base.

c)
Photo 5.40

Photo 5.41 Place the animal on its side and remove the entrails by detaching the large intestine.

a)

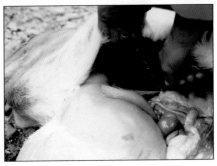

b)

Photo 5.42 (a) Raise the skin of the flank to expose the diaphragm and (b) cut it with the point of your knife.

Photo 5.43 Detach the heart and the liver which are located in the chest cavity.

83

Photo 5.44 Cut the arteries close to the heart to remove it.

Photo 5.45 Remove the liver.

Photo 5.46 After pumping the animal, place it on its belly to allow the blood to flow out.

Optional steps

Photo 5.47 Cut the hide on the sternum.

Photo 5.48 Saw through the sternum.

Photo 5.49 Detach the oesophagus.

MOOSE

Photo 5.50 Detach the penis by cutting the skin on both sides.

Photo 5.51 The scrotum can be removed at the same time as the penis.

Photo 5.52 Cut around the anus and detach six inches (15 cm) of the large intestine, then tie them together.

Photo 5.53 If you plan to have the head mounted, cut the skin on the sternum only.

Photo 5.54 Cut the skin only to the base of the neck. Detach the oesophagus and tie it closed.

Photo 5.55 Use a saw to cut through the sternum, but be careful not to damage the stomach.

Photo 5.56 Cut the skin on the belly right to the anus.

Photo 5.57 The membrane which holds the intestines can be kept to make sausages.

Photo 5.58 Use your free hand to hold the intestines out of the way in order to avoid cutting into them and then cut through the pelvic bone with the tip of your knife.

Photo 5.59 Once the animal is completely spread open, detach the liver which is located not far from the left lung.

Photo 5.60 Here is the liver once it has been removed. This is a healthy liver with no parasites.

Photo 5.61 Once the oesophagus has been tied closed, pull it toward the back of the animal.

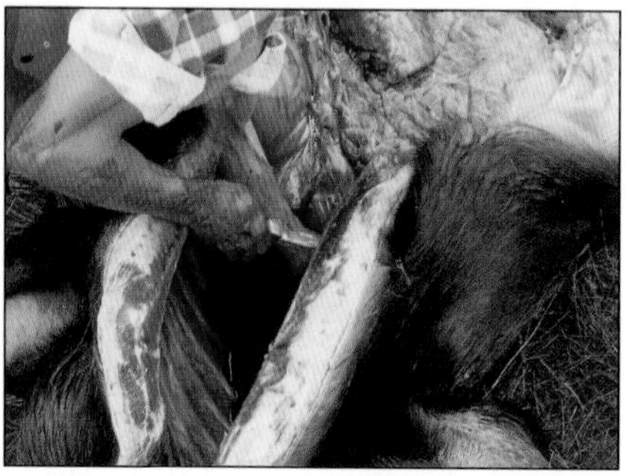

Photo 5.62 Cut through the diaphragm.

Photo 5.63 The inside of the chest cavity is now empty.

88

Photo 5.64 Pull the paunch toward the back of the animal in order to completely remove all the entrails (a & b).

Photo 5.65 Remove the heart.

a)   b)

Photo 5.66 (a) Remove the kidneys and (b) carefully clean away the small globules of fat.

Photo 5.67 After pumping the animal, carefully wipe the inside of the carcass with a clean cloth.

Photo 5.68 The author's father, Lucien LeMay and uncle Leonard Cayouette break into a happy smile, satisfied that the job has been well done.

Practical advice

Tarsal glands

Whitetailed deer, as well as blacktails and mulies, have tarsal glands (photos 5.69) which are located on the inside of the hind legs at the bend. During the rut, these glands give off a strong musky odour. Do not remove these prior to or during the gutting operation since the strong, disagreeable odour will be transferred onto the meat from the knife.

Some hunters use the tarsal glands to cover their scent or attract deer while hunting. If you want to keep the glands, remove them once the animal is skinned and then freeze them. At all costs avoid contaminating the meat by touching the glands.

Photo 5.69 Many hunters remove the tarsal glands and use them to attract other deer. The most common tactic is to rub the glands on the bottom of their hunting boots.

Accidental intestine perforation

If your shot has nicked the intestines or if you accidentally cut them with your knife, do not worry. A couple of pieces of peach or scale paper will quickly fix the problem.

Provided that the stomach or intestinal contents have not spread throughout the interior cavity, cut a few small pieces of peach paper or scale paper and place them over the perforations like dressings. Remove the contents of the abdomen by making an incision between the 11th and 12th rib. On larger game, you will need to make the cut anyway in order to quarter the animal. Once the entrails are removed, meticulously clean the areas soiled with intestinal material using a clean, dampened cloth (cheesecloth). Once the animal is well cooled, remove the fine, transparent membrane which covers the meat. By following these simple steps the meat will not have the unpleasant aftertaste that often results from these mishaps.

Bowhunting?

So you prefer to hunt with bow and arrow or crossbow! Well, the following advice concerning field dressing applies to you in particular.

Often the arrow travels right through the animal and when it does, it is nevertheless important to retrieve the shaft. However, in some cases, the arrow simply buries itself in the animal or, worse yet, breaks off. A finely honed arrow head lodged in the rib cage or abdomen represents serious risks of injury during the process of field dressing.

If the arrow is visible when the animal is recovered, try to remove it using a light pull. If you feel resistance, stop. You can easily remove the arrow later during the cleaning.

When the arrow is not visible, position the animal on its back for field dressing and try to find the entry point. Once you have found the incision, insert a twig in the opening to mark its location. As soon as you have opened the animal, the first task is to find the arrowhead and remove it.

Now, before removing the entrails, use the twig to determine the probable path of the arrow. Once you find it, do not discard it even if it is no longer usable since the blades could cause accidental injury to you or your hunting companions.

Once this operation is completed, field dress the animal following the steps outlined in the previous sections.

Chapter 6

Quartering

The decision on how to quarter a large animal such as a moose or elk depends on three primary factors – the distance to be covered, the physical condition of the hunters and the size of the animal. It is important to accurately and honestly evaluate each of these factors to prevent the task from turning into a nightmare.

A professional person or a business executive cannot be expected to have the same stamina and physical strength as someone who does physical work for a living. Carrying a quarter of a moose for a distance of a mile (1.6 km) can be fatal for some people. Trying to be a hero by volunteering to carry more than you are physically capable of carrying could easily send you to the hospital or, worse, the morgue.

As far as the size of an animal is concerned, it is no coincidence that hunting stories resemble fishing stories in that the animals continue to grow even after they have been packaged and frozen. It is certainly possible to find moose weighing more than half a ton (450 kg), but they represent a very small minority of the animals actually harvested. You can only really and truthfully determine the size of an animal by putting it on a scale. That is why the following table is divided into three categories of moose – 500, 650 and 800 pounds (225, 300 and 360 kg) – corresponding to the actual weight of these animals.

It is also useful to study the bone structure illustrations on pages 72 and 96 to understand and implement the various techniques outlined in this book.

COMPARISON CHART

Weight of the animal	Number of quarters	Location of the cut	Sections	Weight of each section	Proportion of load of each section
500 pounds (225 kg)	4	Between 11th and 12th rib	2 fronts	130 pounds (58.5 kg)	52%
			2 hinds	120 pounds (54 kg)	48%
	6	Between 5th and 6th rib and the 5th and 6th lumbar vertebrae	2 fronts	87.5 pounds (39.4 kg)	35%
			2 loins	75 pounds (34 kg)	30%
			2 hinds	87.5 pounds (39.4 kg)	35%
650 pounds (300 kg)	4	Between 11th and 12th rib	2 fronts	169 pounds (78 kg)	52%
			2 hinds	156 pounds (72 kg)	48%

800 pounds (360 kg)	6	Between 5th rib and 6th rib and the 5th and 6th lumbar vertebrae	2 fronts	113.5 pounds (52.5 kg)	35%
			2 loins	98 pounds (45 kg)	30%
			2 hinds	113.5 pounds (52.5 kg)	35%
	4	Between 11th and 12th rib	2 fronts	208 pounds (94,6 kg)	52%
			2 hinds	192 pounds (87,4 kg)	48%
	6	Between 5th rib and 6th rib and the 5th and 6th lumbar vertebrae	2 fronts	140 pounds (63 kg)	35%
			2 loins	120 pounds (54 kg)	30%
			2 hinds	140 pounds (63 kg)	35%

Quartering the carcass

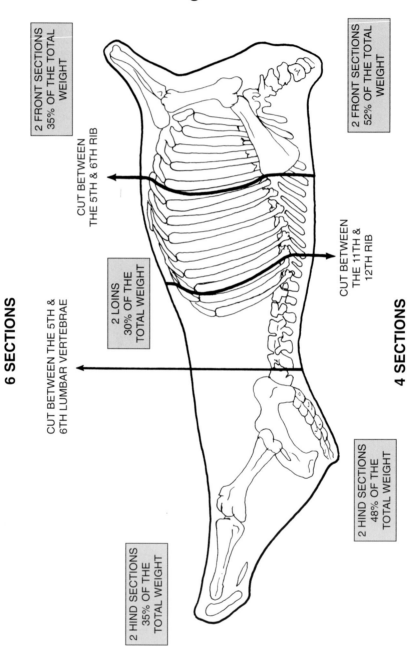

2 FRONT SECTIONS 35% OF THE TOTAL WEIGHT

2 FRONT SECTIONS 52% OF THE TOTAL WEIGHT

CUT BETWEEN THE 5TH & 6TH RIB

CUT BETWEEN THE 11TH & 12TH RIB

2 LOINS 30% OF THE TOTAL WEIGHT

6 SECTIONS

CUT BETWEEN THE 5TH & 6TH LUMBAR VERTEBRAE

4 SECTIONS

2 HIND SECTIONS 48% OF THE TOTAL WEIGHT

2 HIND SECTIONS 35% OF THE TOTAL WEIGHT

Removing the head

It is best to remove the head (photos 6.1, 6.2 and 6.3) before cutting the animal into quarters. In order to get the maximum amount of meat, make your cut at the base of the skull by following the hollow situated behind the ears and a right angle formed by the lower jaw. This cut should be made on both sides of the head.

Four quarters

In order to create the four quarters, first separate the animal into halves by cutting between the 11th and 12th rib on a large animal like a moose or between the 12th and 13th rib on a smaller animal such as a caribou. Once you have located the appropriate ribs, start from the spinal column and work outward, cutting first through the muscle tissue between the ribs, then the skin. Using a saw, cut through the cartilage (the continuation of the ribs) and repeat the operation on the other side. Now you will need to cut through the backbone. Once completed, the carcass will be in two pieces.

Longitudinal cut

In order to separate the front (photo 6.8) and rear halves (photo 6.14) of the carcass, cut down through the backbone following the raised ridges. If possible, place the halves skin side down on top of a stump, the trunk of a fallen tree or a boulder in order to keep them off the ground and to keep them clean.

Once the quarters are sawed in half, you will need to separate the skin with a sharp knife. The closer the saw cuts are to the middle of the vertebrae, the more meat you will get from the animal. A good indication that you have cut the backbone properly is when the channel that houses the spinal cord is cut in half lengthwise.

The cut can also be accomplished with an axe, although having a second axe on hand makes the task easier and reduces the tendency to drift off the centre. It also substantially reduces the number of bone splinters that need to be removed later. The following illustration shows the technique to use. Take your time and you will get a clean cut.

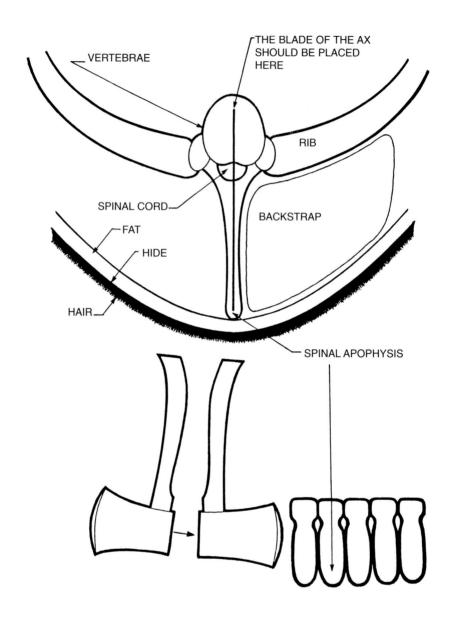

VERTEBRAE

THE BLADE OF THE AX
SHOULD BE PLACED
HERE

RIB

SPINAL CORD

BACKSTRAP

FAT

HIDE

HAIR

SPINAL APOPHYSIS

Cutting the backbone

Place the blade of the ax on the flat of the 11th vertebrae, as close to
the center as possible, hit the head of it with a second ax.

Keeping the cut precisely down the centre of the vertebrae is critical because some of the most tender meat is located along the backbone, including the backstraps. These filets run from the pelvic bone all the way forward to the 13th rib near the shoulder. It is a choice cut of meat and care should be taken not to damage it during the field dressing operation.

Removing the hooves

The hooves can be removed (photos 6.10, 6.11 and 6.13) either before or after the carcass is quartered. The front hooves are removed by cutting through the carpus bones while the rear hooves require cutting at the tarsus bones. First cut the skin completely around the knuckle and bend the foot as far backward as it will go in order to open the joint. Now use your knife to cut through the ligaments which hold the knuckle together and it should separate. In the case of the rear legs, the same technique is used, but be careful not to cut the Achilles tendons because these will be used to suspend the rear quarters.

A saw does the cleanest job and if you do decide to go that route, it is important to cut the hide with a knife in order to avoid clogging the teeth of the saw.

CARIBOU

Photo 6.1 Cut the skin and the muscle tissue as close as possible to the base of the head in order to locate the junction with the neck bones.

Photo 6.2 Separate the occiput (it resembles a billiard ball with a hole in it) and atlas which is the first cervical vertebra.

Photo 6.3 The head dislocated from the neck.

Photo 6.4 Count the ribs starting at the front of the animal.

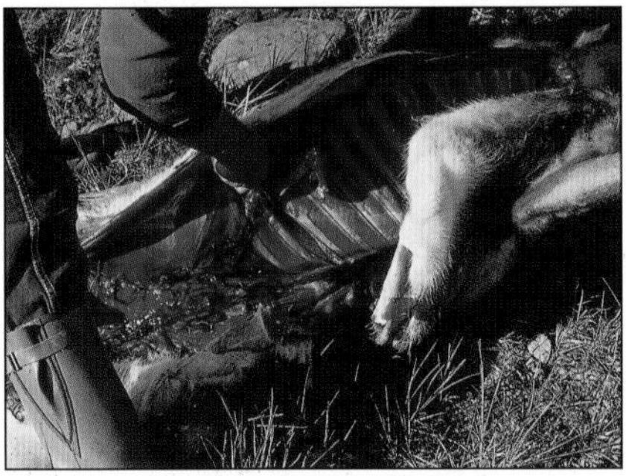

Photo 6.5 From the inside, cut between the 12th and 13th ribs.

Photo 6.6 Do the same on the other side of the carcass.

Photo 6.7 Saw through the backbone in order to separate the front section from the rear section.

Photo 6.8 Separate the front part of the carcass by sawing down the length of the backbone and then cutting the skin with a knife.

Photo 6.9 This is what the front sections should look like once the backbone has been sawed.

Photo 6.10 In order to remove the front hooves, first cut the skin at the middle of the bend.

Photo 6.11 Next, dislocate the lower leg from the upper leg at the bend.

Photo 6.12 Wrap the front sections in cheesecloth.

Photo 6.13 Saw or dislocate the rear legs.

Photo 6.14 Saw through the center of the backbone to separate the rear section of the carcass.

Photo 6.15 Cut the skin of the rear sections with a knife.

Photo 6.16 Cover the rear sections with cheesecloth as well.

Photo 6.17 The carcass is now in manageable sections ready for transport.

MOOSE

Photo 6.18 Cut the skin and the muscle tissue around the neck at the base of the skull.

Photo 6.19 Dislocate the skull at the first cervical vertebra.

Photo 6.20 After having cut the skin with a knife, dislocate or saw through the lower leg bone.

Photo 6.21 Cut the meat and skin between the 11th and 12th ribs.

Photo 6.22 Saw through the cartilage at the extremity of the ribs at right angles to them.

Photo 6.23 Do the same on the other side, again starting at the backbone.

Photo 6.24 Saw through the backbone.

Photo 6.25 Now separate the sides by cutting the backbone lengthwise.

A lighter load

In order to cut the carcass into six parts, make your cut between the fifth and sixth rib right to the backbone using the technique described earlier. Separating the fifth and sixth lumbar vertebrae is much easier because there are no more ribs at this point. As in the case for quartering the carcass, you will need to first cut through the muscle tissue and then the hide. At this stage you should have three segments of the carcass. These are now cut in half to create a total of six parts, which are lighter to transport.

Photo 6.26 Remove the head.

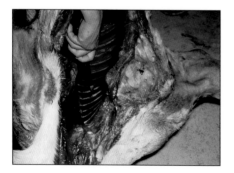

Photo 6.27 Separate the front section of the carcass from the rear section between the 5th and 6th ribs.

Photo 6.28 Do the same on the other side.

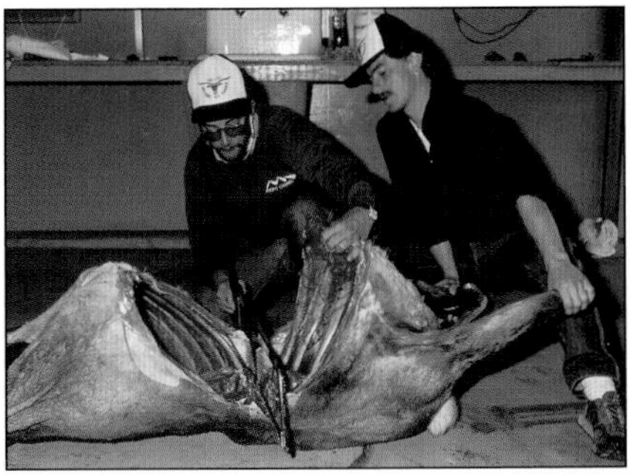

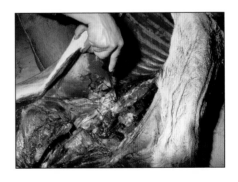

Photo 6.29 Saw through the back-bone.

Photo 6.30 Find the joint between the 5th and 6th lumbar vertebrae.

Photo 6.31 At that point, cut the flanks starting at the backbone.

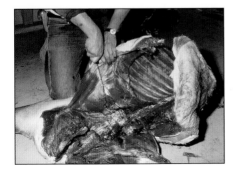

107

Photo 6.32 Repeat this cut on the other side.

Photo 6.33 Cut through the backbone to separate the loins from the legs.

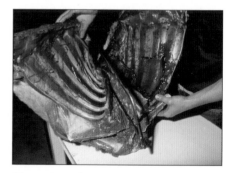

Photo 6.34 Separate the front section by sawing through the center of the backbone.

a)

b)

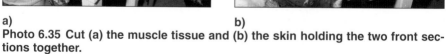

Photo 6.35 Cut (a) the muscle tissue and (b) the skin holding the two front sections together.

Photo 6.36 Repeat the operation on the other side.

Carrying them out

At this point, the task of carrying out the carcass starts in earnest. The technique used for moose and elk is slightly different than that used for deer and caribou.

Moose and elk quarters can be carried on the shoulders for short distances, but a backpack with a tumpline is more convenient and less tiring. If there is no tumpline available, make an incision in the hide of the animal to create a built-in tump. A pack board to which the quarter can be firmly attached also works well, making the job easier.

For smaller game like deer, a sling is ideal. Attach the hind legs to the poles, and then tie the front legs behind the head before attaching them to the sling. Make sure the animal is firmly tied to the pole to prevent it from swaying.

Avoid dragging the animal for any long distance because this will damage the meat to the point where the backstraps actually detach. If you only need to go a short distance, attach the front legs to the head and then drag the animal by the antlers (photo 6.37).

Caribou are usually separated into four quarters for transport. If the animal is of medium size, the carcass can simply be separated into three parts – head, front portion, hind portion.

It is a good idea to tie a bright piece of fabric, particularly fluorescent orange, to the carcass or the quarters while transporting (photo 6.38) it out of the bush in order to avoid being mistaken for game by other hunters.

All-terrain vehicles make the task of transporting an animal out of the bush almost too easy. Simply make a series of small incisions in the hide and pass a cord through them in order to attach the animal firmly to the carrying rack of the ATV (photo 6.39). In marshy areas, it is a good idea to cover it with a sheet of polyethylene (photo 6.40). But be careful because if the animal is still warm, in order to reduce the risk of spoiling, it should not be covered for any extended period of time.

If you do use an ATV, please respect other hunters in the region.

Photo 6.37 Because of the rocky ground in the tundra, a caribou should not be dragged for more than a very short distance.

Photo 6.38 This is the safe way to transport game. Note the orange cloth over the quarter.

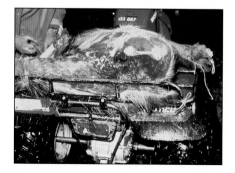

Photo 6.39 The quarters of a moose firmly attached to the rack of an all-terrain vehicle.

Photo 6.40 A moose quarter covered with a plastic sheet to protect it from the rain.

We cannot insist enough the importance of taking your time when you are quartering the carcass. The photos and illustrations will help you make the right cuts so that the task is relatively simple. Refer to them often if necessary and remember that a hasty job is rarely well done. The amount of meat you get back from the butcher depends on how good a job you do.

In case of rain

When it is raining, most hunters tend to put away their guns and get together for a game of cards in front of the fire. Nevertheless, you will find the more avid hunters out in the bush telling themselves that the season is already far too short to waste a day indoors. If you fall into the latter category there is a good chance you will fill your tag sooner or later. However, be sure to place the quarters in such a way that the hide is on top, to keep the rain off the meat (as opposed to

Photo 6.41 Moose quarters protected from the rain under a plastic shelter.

dry weather when the quarters should be placed skin side down so that they can cool quicker). Above all, do not cover the quarters with a plastic sheet or tarp.

However, if you manage to encounter your trophy relatively close to camp, needing only a short haul, the best solution is to hang the quarters up and then create a lean-to using a tarp to protect the meat from the rain and ensuring proper air circulation around the quarters (photo 6.41).

Shelters

It takes some ingenuity to prevent bears, wolves, coyotes and foxes from making a meal out of your hard-won venison.

If you are close to a body of water, you can anchor a boat a good distance from shore and place the meat in it out of harm's way. If you do not have two boats, do not forget to attach a rope to the boat so that you can later pull it to shore.

If you need to leave the carcass in the bush, clear a circular area around it of all underbrush, making sure that the gut pile is outside the circle. In addition, leave an article of clothing close to the carcass since human scent will keep predators away. A blinking lantern will also work surprisingly well.

One of the best options is to hang the meat out of reach of predators. The only problem is that birds quickly find them and peck away at the quarters, especially the fatty tissues. This can be minimized to some degree, by covering the meat in cheesecloth bags. Canada (grey) jays and magpies tend to be a bit more aggressive.

On hunting trips to remote regions, it is not always possible to head back to civilization once the animal has been tagged. In order to protect the quarters from the sun, flies and birds, a screened shelter becomes a necessity. It should be square or rectangular in shape, and six to nine feet in length (2 to 3 m) depending on the number of animals to be stored in it. The frame as well as the lower portion can be made from logs but the upper portion should measure four to six feet (1.7 to 2 m) and be covered with screening. A plastic or fabric tarpaulin can be used for the roof, but do not use clear or semi-clear plastic since this will allow the heat of the sun to pass through. Of course, a meat house which can be disassembled and left in place for the following season is particularly practical if you hunt in the same area year after year. It is a good idea to check the regulations before you go to that trouble, since in many cases such buildings are dismantled in freehold or leased territories.

Chapter 7

Variety meats

Depending on where you are from, the edible organs of animals are known as variety meats, organ meats and, if your origins are in Great Britain, you are probably familiar with the term offal. By definition, these are the meats taken from parts other than the skeletal muscles and they include a wide range of organs including the heart, kidneys, liver and tongue. To the true gourmet, these are indeed delicacies that deserve to be treasured and savoured while others are not nearly as passionate about them. The fact is that game variety meats properly cared for and prepared are excellent fare worth the extra bit of attention.

As previously mentioned, the liver, heart and kidneys are normally removed and set aside during the course of the field dressing. The two other items of interest, the tongue and brain, can be removed once back at camp. If you do intend to keep either of both of these organs, it is important to treat the head of the animal like you would any other portion, making sure that it is cooled properly and kept clean until you are ready to remove the items.

Unlike other meats, these items require no aging. In fact, the faster they are cooled and kept cool, the more they retain their nutritional values and the better they taste. If you opt to eat them at a later date, be sure to freeze the items in appropriate freezer bags (photo 7.1). Whenever possible, freeze the tongue, heart and kidneys whole. The liver, on the other hand, can be cut into smaller, meal-sized portions and just prior to cooking these can be cut into slices while still half frozen.

Photo 7.1 Freeze any organ meat which you will not eat right away.

Photo 7.2 After having cut and removed the skin under the lower jaw, pull out the tongue, cutting the cartilage which hold it in place.

Photo 7.3 Clean the tongue in water and scrape it, starting at the tip, to remove any plant residues (a & b). (Except for bulls in rut, almost all animals have particles of food in their mouths).

Photo 7.4 Trim away the cartilage found under the thickest part of the tongue.

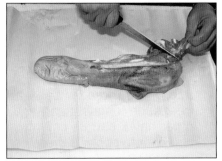

Photo 7.5 Remove the membrane on either side.

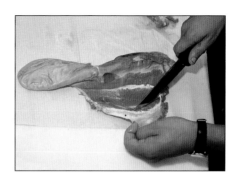

Photo 7.6 The tongue is now ready to be cooked. Rich in proteins and minerals, this is a considered a delicacy.

Photo 7.7 Remove the membrane that covers the kidneys as well as the white tissue in the center in order to eliminate the disagreeable odour usually associated with this organ meat.

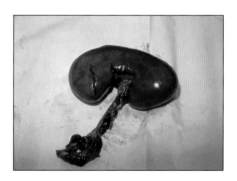

Photo 7.8 Slice the kidneys if you plan to eat them immediately.

Photo 7.9 This is the heart before being cleaned.

a)

b)

Photo 7.10 (a) Thoroughly empty out the heart to ensure that there is no coagulated blood at the bottom, then (b) trim away the fat from the outside.

a)

b)

Photo 7.11 After making a small incision in the membrane with the tip of your knife, (a) slide your finger under the membrane and (b) remove it by pulling upwards. Only remove the membrane from the portion which will be eaten immediately.

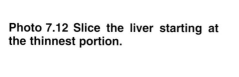**Photo 7.12 Slice the liver starting at the thinnest portion.**

The recipes

While it is true that not everyone is keen on variety meats, those who are accustomed to eating beef or pork livers are always surprised by the delicate and wonderful flavour of game organs. Here are a few easy ideas on preparing these items. They are sure to be appreciated.

Tongue

The tongue of big game animals is excellent. Unfortunately, most hunters leave this item for the coyotes and foxes.

First, soak the tongue in a solution of three parts cold water and one part vinegar. Next, cook in boiling water. Once the tongue is cooked, the skin covering it comes off easily.

Tongue can be eaten cold or hot. In the latter case, slice the tongue like you would a roast and sauté in a hot pan.

Kidneys

Many people have an aversion to eating kidney, primarily because, at some point in their lives, they were served kidney which had not been properly cleaned. It is critical to trim away all the vessels in the core of the kidney before cooking to eliminate the odour of urine. If you want to take additional precautions, you can also soak the trimmed kidneys for four hours in a mixture consisting of one part vinegar and three parts cold water.

Once that is done, either cut them into slices and sauté them in a hot pan. Deglaze the pan with some red wine and pour the resulting liquid over the slices.

Liver

Except in rare circumstances, the liver of big game animals is very tender. In order to retain that tenderness, it is important not to overcook it. Cut the liver into thin slices, ⅜ inch (1 cm).

Dredge the slices in a beaten egg and then in flour. Sear quickly over medium heat on both sides. The centre should remain slightly pink.

Enjoy!

Chapter 8

Transporting the meat

The weight and size of the quarters are important considerations when you are transporting a large animal some distance out of a remote location, either by muscle power or by float plane. Under these circumstances, it is preferable to cut the animal into smaller, lighter pieces.

The following sequence of photographs demonstrates how the weight can be easily and quickly reduced. As you can see, it is just a matter of deboning certain parts of the animal while leaving the skin on.

Preparing the front sections

Photo 8.1 Remove the bruised tissues as well as all meat that was damaged by the shot.

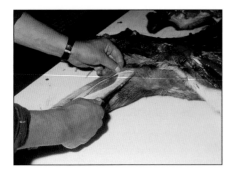

Photo 8.2 Split the skin along the shinbones (radius and ulna).

Photo 8.3 Cut along the bones with the tip of your knife.

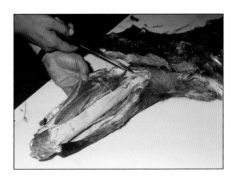

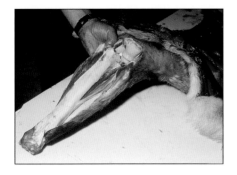

Photo 8.4 Dislocate them from the shoulder bone.

Photo 8.5 Completely debone the radius and ulna with the tip of your knife.

122

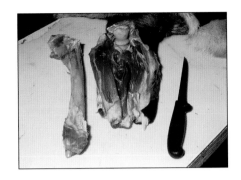

Photo 8.6 This is what the leg should look like once it has been deboned.

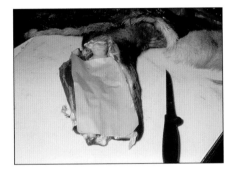

Photo 8.7 Line the inside of the leg with peach paper.

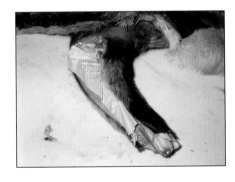

Photo 8.8 Close the cut.

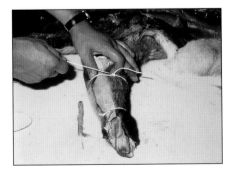

Photo 8.9 Tie it closed with two or three strings.

Preparing the legs

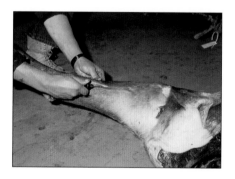

Photo 8.10 Split the skin by cutting along the upper side of the tibia.

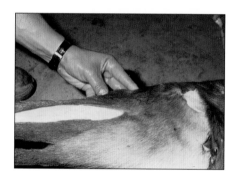

Photo 8.11 Extend the cut right to the joint of the leg where the tibia and femur meet.

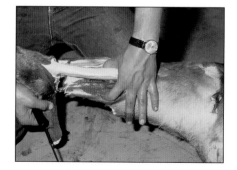

Photo 8.12 Cut the Achilles tendon (hamstring).

Photo 8.13 Completely debone the tibia.

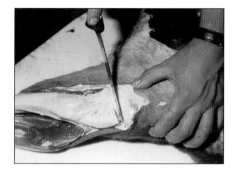

Photo 8.14 Dislocate the tibia at the femur.

Photo 8.15 The joint once it has been dislocated.

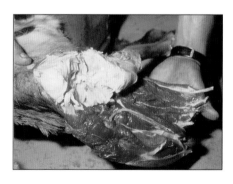

Photo 8.16 The leg with the tibia removed.

Photo 8.17 Line the exposed meat with peach paper.

Photo 8.18 Tie closed with string.

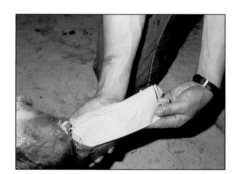

Preparing the full loins

Photo 8.19 The width of your hand provides a good gauge for the cut. Measure out from the back bone.

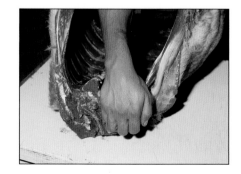

Photo 8.20 Saw the ribs along the entire length parallel to the backbone, a hand's width away. Repeat on the other side.

Photo 8.21 Place peach paper over the backbone and fold back the flank.

Photo 8.22 Also line the flank which has been folded back with peach paper.

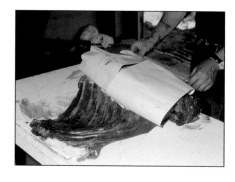

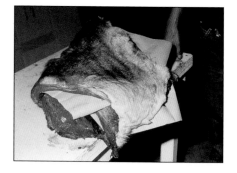

Photo 8.23 Fold the first flank over the second flank.

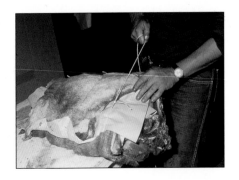

Photo 8.24 Tie into a compact package with cord.

Bear in mind that meat which has not completely cooled is much more difficult to manipulate and this is especially the case when it has been partly deboned. Hence, it is preferable to let the meat cool completely. Ideally you should wait at least 24 hours after the animal has been killed before undertaking the trip out of the bush.

Chapter 9

Parasites & diseases

As is the case with domestic animals, all wild animals, particularly the deer family, are liable to have parasites. There are many different types of parasites and they differ as much in shape as they do in their methods of reproduction and the tissues in which they are found. They also vary in their degree of danger to man. Some parasites, especially liver flukes and tuberculosis bacteria are pathogenic in that they are responsible for serious illnesses.

Rather than try to provide an encyclopaedia of parasites, we will take a look at the parasites you are most likely to come across as well as some of the other problems a hunter is liable to encounter. It is a point worth remembering that the liver of an animal is most likely the first organ to become diseased and, as such, is a good indicator of its health. If the liver looks healthy and shows no sign of being infected by disease, there is a good chance the animal was healthy with very little if any infection in other organs.

Tapeworm

Tapeworms (photo 9.1) are most frequently encountered in moose. These parasitic worms are usually found as small cysts about the size of a match head, usually off-white or yellowish in colour, in the muscle tissues of an animal.

Both cooking and freezing kill the parasites. If you do find some of the cysts, simply remove them; the meat is still edible. However, if the meat is infested with a large number of the cysts, you should contact a biologist.

Liver flukes

Liver flukes (photo 9.2) are most often encountered in caribou. The surface of an infected liver is usually dotted with whitish welts or swellings and, when you cut the liver open, you will usually see greenish marbling. In both cases, the liver should not be consumed, but the meat of the animal is edible.

Hydatid cysts

Hydatid cysts (photo 9.3) are generally round, off-white or sometimes bluish in colour and can vary in size from the diameter of a dime to a quarter. You will find them in the liver, lungs and muscle tissue. The meat of the animal is edible provided it is cooked properly, but the cysts can be un-appetizing, so we suggest removing them whenever found. In doing so, be careful not to perforate the sac because it contains a clear liquid full of small white granules which will contaminate the surrounding meat.

Warble fly

The larvae of the warble fly (photo 9.4) are most commonly seen on caribou. They develop on the back of the animal, specifically in the fat of the back. They usually look like a small brown shell with one end somewhat pointed. The parasites can be as large as a 25-cent piece. Simply remove them; they pose no danger to humans.

Tuberculosis

On most members of the deer family, tuberculosis is usually seen as off-white or yellowish pea-sized lumps behind the flat side of the liver, particularly along the main vein.

Even when only a few of these lumps are found, you should always wear gloves during the field dressing and also carefully examine the condition of the liver. If you do come across the telltale lumps, contact your game department or animal health agency before bringing the meat to a butcher. Many jurisdictions will recommend the animal be safely disposed of and a replacement permit may be issued.

Photo 9.1 Tapeworm nodes.

Photo 9.2 Liver flukes.

Photo 9.3 Hydatid cysts.

Photo 9.4 Warble fly larva.

Photo 9.5 Abscess.

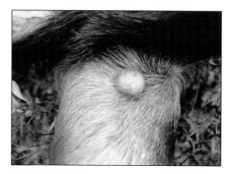

Photo 9.6 Warts.

Abscesses

Abscesses (photo 9.5) are rarely found on wild game. These pockets of greenish pus are usually found in the muscle tissues of the animal. They should be carefully removed and you should disinfect all equipment that has come in contact with the pocket. Only the infected parts of the animal should be discarded, the rest of the animal is edible.

Warts

As the name implies, warts (photo 9.6) are found on the skin of animals, most often around the neck and shoulders. The warts are usually round and can be as big as golf balls. They are actually benign tumours and not cancerous. In order to remove them, simply cut through the narrow stem that attaches them to the skin. The presence of warts has absolutely no effect on the quality of the meat.

Hunters who encounter these or any other wildlife diseases and want to know more about them should contact their game department or a government veterinary centre.

Chronic wasting disease

Animals suffering from chronic wasting disease (CWD) are generally unconcerned over the approach of a hunter and show signs of malnourishment, excessive salivation, trembling, unsteadiness and a lack of coordination. They also have difficulty in chewing and are perpetually thirsty, urinating often as a result.

A number of cases have been reported in the Midwestern US, in Alberta and in Saskatchewan. Elk, mule deer and whitetailed deer seem to be most at risk. In order to monitor the problem, farmed animals as well as those in zoos are kept under careful observation.

According to the World Health Organization, there is currently not proof that CWD is transmissible to humans. Nevertheless, I think it is wise to abstain from consuming the brain of game animals.

Cadmium

Cadmium is one of several heavy metal elements. It is

produced by pollution and, as a result of a chemical transformation, it is deposited on vegetation which is, in turn, consumed by plant-eating animals, including deer, elk, moose and caribou. The liver and kidneys serve as filters for the blood and so this is where the cadmium accumulates.

In some areas of the east coast, the amount of cadmium found in samples is three times the level recommended for human consumption in a normal portion of five ounces (140 g). As a result, it is advisable to abstain from consuming the liver and kidneys.

Government agencies

The United States Department of Agriculture (USDA) and the Canadian Food Inspection Agency (CFIA) oversee human and animal health in their respective areas. There is constant communication between the two agencies as well as various other organizations and government departments. If and when a major disease risk develops or erupts, these different organizations issue public alerts, advising their populations of the problem.

Various government departments have published brochures explaining the diseases, parasites and other problems affecting animals and fish.

Butchers who specialize in game can advise you. The veterinarian associated with the butcher, a wildlife biologist or the regional office of a government agency (wildlife service, natural resources or agriculture) should be in a position to provide answers or at least be able to direct you to someone who can answer your concerns.

Chapter 10

Your trophy

So you have had a wonderful hunt, great companionship, memorable experiences in the outdoors and you have managed to tag out on a trophy animal. There is plenty of prime venison to grace your table for many months to come and antlers for your wall to remind you of the good times you had.

If you are planning to have your trophy mounted, you will find useful information on the following pages regarding the proper procedure for caping the head and making sure the skin reaches the taxidermist in the best possible condition.

The only way to treat the skin in the bush is to salt it. This entails vigorously rubbing coarse salt into the hide as soon as you have skinned the animal. If there are pieces of fat on the skin, remove these before salting. If you plan to keep the skin whole, fold the sides toward the centre once the hide is salted. Now fold it again, still in the same direction. Finally, roll it up into a tight package. When you arrive at home, remove the first application of salt that has become wet from the skin and then apply fresh salt before rolling up the hide once more. We recommend as many re-applications of salt as time will allow because each application further ensures that the hair will not fall.

If you do not intend to have the skin or cape tanned right away, simply wrap it well so that it does not leak and freeze it. Once frozen, the skin will keep for several months.

The head

If you plan to have the head mounted, you will need to take that into account when you are field dressing the animal.

Photo 10.1 This is how much skin should be left attached to the head in order to get an appealing mount and make the taxidermist's job easier.

As previously mentioned, the skin should be cut no farther than the point of the sternum, rather than up to the point of the jaw. Once you have finished removing the entrails, continue cutting the skin by following an imaginary line up along the shoulders to the back. In the case of a bull moose, the cut should be made to the start of the hump (photos 10.2 and 10.3).

Now cut the skin along the top of the neck rather than underneath it, to a point two to four inches (5 to 10 cm) back from the point of the skull. If conditions allow and the flies are not too bad, skin out the neck right to the base of the lower jaw. Now cut through the joint that attaches the head to the neck to detach it. In the case of a moose, this operation will save you 10 to 17 pounds (5 to 8 kg) of meat and it can be carried out in the forest. However, since the surface will dry out to some degree, be prepared for some loss of meat. In

Photo 10.2 The hide of a trophy white-tailed deer cut along the back of the neck.

Photo 10.3 This is what it looks like.

any case, it is critical to remove the oesophagus and windpipe and then cover the neck with cheesecloth.

Unless you have caped out game before, skinning out the head should be left to the taxidermist. If you must do the caping in order to reduce the weight, proceed with extreme caution since every nick in the hide will make it more difficult for the taxidermist to produce a perfect mount.

To remove the cape from the head, start by making a Y-cut from the back of the head to the bases of the antlers. Carefully work the skin away from the antlers and then gradually remove the cape like a glove by cutting the connective tissue as close as possible to the skull. Work carefully around the ears, eyes, the mouth and the nose. Remove the cartilage from the ears and then rub salt meticulously into the skin, leaving no area bare. Finally, roll up the cape. The antlers can be removed from the skull by sawing through the skull plate parallel to the lower jaw using an imaginary line that runs through the centre of the eyes.

The antlers

Carrying out the antlers without the head makes things much easier (photos 10.4 to 10.7). If the antlers are too big and must be cut for transport, saw the skull plate between the two bases from the inside, being careful not to damage the cape. Now, attach the two antlers together so that the skin will not split or tear (if you keep only the antlers).

Photo 10.4 With a knife, cut the skin behind the antlers, about 4 inches (10 cm) down.

a)

b)

Photo 10.5 (a) Continue the cut in line with the center of the eye and parallel to the lower jaw and then (b) about halfway between the nose and the eye. Follow the same points of reference around the other side of the skull to meet the initial cut at the back of the antlers.

Photo 10.6 Saw the skull following the cuts made above.

Photo 10.7 The task of removing the antler is complete.

Remember that the preliminary work on the head of a trophy requires a great deal of care. One accidental slip of knife or a cape that has not been properly cared for makes the work of a taxidermist considerably more difficult. It also makes the difference between an exceptional mount and a disappointing one.

Conclusion

Like many other forms of recreation, hunting allows us to escape the hectic pace of everyday life and clear our minds of the complicated webs that gather. Spending time in the outdoors is the perfect way to rejuvenate and renew mind and soul.

Hunting also allows us to harvest game. It would however be a mistake to calculate the profitability of any trip by dividing the money spent by the weight of the meat obtained. Whether you manage to get your game by skill or luck, it is your responsibility to take the best possible care of the meat. I am convinced that the techniques discussed throughout this book will help you bring your animal to the butcher in the best possible condition. There is no justification for a loss of meat and that is a good reason to put the techniques outlined here into practice. With this information, your outing will not only be enriched by your experiences, but also by the venison you place on the table. Whether you share the meat with friends or family, your efforts in the field will be that much more appreciated.

To end on a slightly different note, we would like to emphasize the importance of registering your game at a wildlife control station as soon as you leave your hunting area, if that is required in the jurisdiction where you hunt. Registering big game animals, including bears, might be required by law and it demonstrates excellent cooperation between hunters and biologists. In effect, the biologists rely on this cooperation in order to keep an eye on the health of our game animals; they also count on you to provide them with samples of liver, heart, lungs, kidneys and ovaries. This cooperation will only help maintain the condition of our big game herds and raise the sport of hunting to the level it deserves.

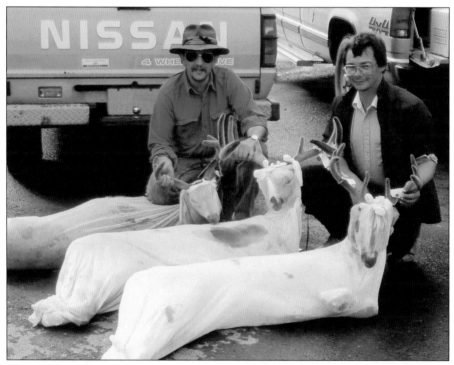

Even during early-season hunts when the weather tends to be mild, there are ways to keep venison cool. Shown here are the author and his hunting partner, Guy Charrette.